WORLD KITCHEN
ITALY

WORLD KITCHEN
ITALY

MURDOCH BOOKS

CONTENTS

THE BEAUTY OF ITALY'S FOOD IS IN ITS GASTRONOMIC DIVERSITY. EACH AREA IS LOYAL TO ITS SPECIALITIES, AND INGREDIENTS AND RECIPES CHANGE FROM THE MOUNTAINS TO THE COAST, FROM THE SOUTH TO THE NORTH, AND THE MAINLAND TO THE ISLANDS.

This regionality is historically attributed to the individualism of the sovereign states that made up Italy until the nineteenth century; to foreign influences; and to the geography that saw rice and polenta grow in the North, wild boar find a home in the forests of central Italy and tomatoes and eggplants (aubergines) prosper in the sunbaked South.

Before the Second World War, Italy could be divided up geographically by its cuisine: the North cooked with butter, polenta, risotto and stewed meats; the Centre ate lard and fresh pasta; and the South lived on olive oil, dried pasta, pizza, chilli and tomatoes. In the past fifty years, with the movement of people from the South to the North and from the country to the city, this has changed.

Yet cucina regionale (regional food) is still very much alive. Despite industrialization and the changing face of the countryside, the artisanal skills that are the foundation for cucina regionale remain, and there is pride in the production of local foods like cheese, ham, oil and pasta. Wine is also a regional speciality – at many restaurants, the choice is simply between a carafe of local red or white.

Italy is also the home of the Slow Food Movement, which champions the cause of regional food and tradition. Indeed, the whole country is undergoing a nostalgia for regional cooking and for cucina povera (the food of poorer southern Italy). Even in restaurants that don't specialize in regional food, dishes with traditional ingredients such as beans, chestnuts, grains and wild salad leaves are popular.

Eating and drinking well is a national pastime, from selecting fresh vegetables in the market to having a mid-morning espresso in a café, lunching in a simple trattoria, and picking up some antipasto from the salumeria on the way home from work.

To many Italians, food shopping is practically a full-time job. Shops open twice a day so you can buy once for lunch and again for dinner. Every city, town and village has at least one market, where produce is seasonal and standards are high as stalls compete for shoppers.

Apart from the alimentari (general stores), there are a number of specialized food shops you would expect to find in every Italian town:

- The caseificio and latteria sell dairy products and often eggs. These can be part of the dairy itself.
- The enoteca sells wine, by the bottle and also often by volume from huge containers.
- The macelleria (butcher) sells meat and poultry.
- The norcineria, named for the famed butchers of Norcia, sells salumi (cured pork products).
- The salumeria also sells salumi, along with fresh pasta and speciality items.
- The panificio, panetteria and forno sell breads and baked goods. They bake twice a day, once for each opening.
- The pasticceria sell pastries.
- The pescheria is the fishmonger.
- The rosticceria is a very upmarket take-away, selling spit-roast chickens, meat and other prepared foods.

- The frantoio is an olive oil mill or a shop that sells olive oil. The oil can be bought by the tin, bottle or by volume like wine.
- The gelateria is the ice cream shop, often doing a take-away trade in cartons, as well as cones and cups.

Italians love to buy from the source, and vineyards, cheese-, pasta- and salumi-makers often have shops where you can buy straight from the producer. Mozzarella can be purchased from the dairy while still warm, pasta bought by the kilo at the factory, balsamic vinegar direct from the acetaia and fish off boats.

Cafés and bars are another mainstay of Italian life. In small towns they are the focus of the square and they are usually occupied by a row of men drinking espresso or small shots from the bar. In and around Naples, your espresso may be sweetened by the barista, while in other areas it is left up to you. Cappuccino is considered more to be breakfast than a drink and is never drunk after eleven in the morning.

THE FOOD OF THE NORTH

Encompassing Piemonte, Valle d'Aosta, Lombardia and Liguria in the northwest and Trentino-Alto Adige, Veneto and Friuli-Venezia Giulia in the northeast, the food of the North has been shaped by the influence of its northern neighbours and mountainous terrain. Polenta and rice are staples, and its dairy products and wines are considered among Italy's best.

Piemonte is home to the highly prized white Alba truffle, sprinkled over melted fontina in Piemonte's fondue-like fonduta, over pasta or eggs. Pastries are served in Turin's famous cafés, while Alba is famed for fine chocolate. This region also produces Italy's best grissini and some of its greatest wines, including Barolo and Barbaresco.

The mountainous Valle d'Aosta is most famous for its alpine cheeses, especially fontina, Toma and Robiola, which are central to the region's cuisine.

Lombardia has a very diverse cuisine. Many of Italy's finest cheeses, such as Gorgonzola, Taleggio, Bel Paese and Grana Padano are produced here, and fresh pasta, polenta and rice are all enjoyed, including the classic risotto alla milanese. To the north, Valtellina is famed for bresaola (air-dried beef) and pizzoccheri, a buckwheat pasta.

Ligurian cuisine is unusual in northern Italy for its use of basil, most notably in pesto alla genovese. This is eaten with trenette, tagliatelle-like noodles, gnocchi and in minestrone. The mountains behind the Riviera provide herbs for cooking. Specialities are focaccia and walnut sauce.

Trentino-Alto Adige can be gastronomically divided into two. Alto Adige is Austrian Italy and the cuisine includes speck (cured ham), canederli (dumplings) and gulasch. Trentino is more Italian, though canederli are popular, and the excellent apples of this region are made into a local strudel. Polenta and breads accompany meals.

Outside Venice, the food of Veneto is generally simple, from bean soups, such as pasta e fagioli, to risotto or risi e bisi. Venice is known for its unfussy preparation of seafood. Veneto is also one of Italy's great wine regions, making Bardolino, Valpolicella and Soave.

Friuli-Venezia Giulia, bordering Austria and Slovenia, is known for its prosciutto di San Daniele, an exquisite sweet ham.

THE FOOD OF THE CENTRE
The centre of Italy encompasses Emilia-Romagna, Le Marche, Tuscany and Umbria – some of the best-known gastronomic regions of Italy. This is an area of fresh pasta, great cheeses and salumi and robust wines.

Emilia-Romagna, stretching out west from the Adriatic, is renowned as the country's greatest region for food and produces some of Italy's best-known foods. Prosciutto di Parma is produced south of Parma and often served wafer-thin with bread, while the culatello, mortadella and prosciutto cotto of this area are all well known. Parmigiano Reggiano is eaten in chunks or grated over Emilia-Romagna's wonderful fresh egg pasta, which comes in more shapes and varieties than anywhere else in Italy and includes the region's favourite, tortellini.

Fresh pasta is often served with Emilia-Romagna's ragù, reinterpreted worldwide as Bolognese. Aceto balsamico tradizionale di Modena is an exceptional vinegar, still made in limited quantities by ancient methods that produce an intense flavour.

Le Marche is a self-sufficient area, separated from the rest of central Italy by the Apennines. It is renowned for its Adriatic seafood, used to make local versions of brodetto, a rich fish stew. The local cuisine also makes use of fennel, white and black truffles, and wild mushrooms. Famed dishes include porchetta (roast suckling pig) and vincisgrassi (lasagne made with chicken livers and prosciutto).

Tuscan cooking is recognised as some of Italy's simplest. The world's finest extra virgin olive oils are made here, served drizzled over Tuscany's unsalted bread. Meals are centred around meat, especially beef, soups such as ribollita and papa al pomodoro, and many bean dishes. Tuscans, in fact, are known as i mangiafagioli – the bean-eaters. Siena has its spicy cakes, pan pepato and panforte, that date back to medieval times, while Florence is famous for bistecca alla fiorentina. Tuscany's wines are exceptional, with Chianti being Italy's most famous red.

Umbria is the only landlocked region in Italy, and its food is hearty and simple. There are, however, some outstanding local products, especially the local truffles, wild mushrooms and great pecorino cheeses. The region is most famous for its use of pork – the town of Norcia gave its name to norcineria, meaning pork butcher – and its tiny lentils from Castelluccio.

THE FOOD OF THE SOUTH
Lazio, Abruzzo, Molise, Campania, Puglia, Basilicata, Calabria, Sicily and Sardinia make up Italy's South, home to robust cucina povera (peasant cooking) and a wonderful cuisine that was created from whatever was available: sun-ripened vegetables and fruit, wheat for dried pasta and local cheeses.

Surrounding Rome, Lazio is influenced by the unique food of its capital. Roman cuisine is not delicate and makes use of pasta, beans, artichokes, meat and offal. Its spaghetti alla carbonara and bucatini all'amatriciana both include the local guanciale (cured pig's cheek).

Abruzzo and Molise are mountainous areas with strong rural cooking traditions. Molise produces fine lentils, pasta and olive oils, while saffron is grown in Abruzzo, along with the diavolilli (tiny red chillies) that go into so many dishes.

The cuisine of Campania and Naples is famous throughout the world: spaghetti with tomatoes and basil, spaghetti alle vongole, pizza topped with fresh mozzarella and eggplant (aubergine) Parmigiana. As well as fresh mozzarella, there is good ricotta, goat's cheeses and caciocavallo. Lemons are used in granite and limoncello.

Puglia has had many invaders, but the food remains quintessentially Italian. Here orecchiette is served with cime di rapa (turnip greens) and good cheeses include caciocavallo and pecorino.

Basilicata is one of the poorest regions of Italy, but its cucina povera, dominated by pasta and vegetables, can be delicious. Dishes and meats are spiced with peperoncino.

At the tip of Italy, Calabria has two coastlines, giving it plenty of seafood, particularly swordfish and tuna. Citrus fruit grow well, as do figs and olives. Peperoncino adds fire to the cooking and there is excellent provolone and caciocavallo.

Sicilian food has long been influenced by invaders, particularly the Arabs who brought sugar. The island's dolci (sweets), granite and gelati are still considered Italy's best. There is also plentiful seafood, citrus fruit, and capers for caponata. The Sardinians have traditionally looked more to their interior for food than to their coast. The cuisine is based on sucking pig and lamb, pecorino, pane carasu (flat bread) and honey.

Chapter 1

ANTIPASTO, SALADS AND SOUPS

Antipasto ('before the meal') platters, both hot and cold, include a selection of cured meat, seafood or vegetables of contrasting colours, flavours and textures. Soups and salads use the freshest ingredients from the market.

FRITTO MISTO DI MARE

Mixed Fried Seafood

Fritto misto is traditionally a mixed platter. We usually think of this as seafood, as in this recipe, but fritto misto is one of those Italian dishes that varies from region to region. Some favour meat or vegetables, others use fruit and even chocolate.

250 g (9 oz) baby squid
12 large prawns (shrimp)
8 small octopus
16 scallops, cleaned
12 fresh sardines, gutted and heads removed
250 g (9 oz) firm white fish fillets (such as ling, cod or snapper), skinned and cut into large cubes
oil, for deep-frying
lemon wedges

GARLIC AND ANCHOVY SAUCE
125 ml (4 fl oz/½ cup) extra virgin olive oil
2 garlic cloves, crushed
3 anchovy fillets, finely minced
2 tablespoons finely chopped flat-leaf (Italian) parsley
pinch of chilli flakes

BATTER
200 g (7 oz/1⅔ cups) plain (all-purpose) flour
¼ teaspoon salt
80 ml (3 fl oz/⅓ cup) olive oil
1 large egg white

Preheat the oven to 140°C (275°F/Gas 1). Clean the squid by pulling the heads and tentacles out of the bodies along with any innards. Cut the heads off below the eyes, just leaving the tentacles. Discard the heads and set the tentacles aside. Rinse the bodies, pulling out the clear quills, and cut the bodies into rings. Peel and devein the prawns, leaving the tails intact.

Clean the octopus by slitting the head and pulling out the innards. Cut out the eyes and hard beak and rinse. If the octopus are large, cut them into halves or quarters. Dry all of the seafood on paper towels so the batter will stick.

To make the sauce, warm the oil in a frying pan. Add the garlic, anchovy, parsley and chilli. Cook over low heat for 1 minute, or until the garlic is soft but not brown. Serve warm or chilled.

To make the batter, sift the flour and salt into a bowl. Mix in the oil with a wooden spoon, then gradually add 315 ml (11 fl oz/1¼ cups) tepid water, changing to a whisk when the mixture is liquid and whisking until the batter is smooth and thick. Stiffly whisk the egg white and fold into the batter. Heat the oil in a deep-fat fryer or deep frying pan to 190°C (375°F), or until a piece of bread fries golden brown in 10 seconds when dropped in the oil.

Working with one type of seafood at a time, dip the pieces in batter. Shake off the excess batter, then carefully lower into the oil. Deep-fry for 2–3 minutes. Drain on paper towels, then transfer to the oven while you fry the remaining seafood.

Serve the seafood immediately with the lemon wedges and the sauce.

SERVES 4

Bruschetta al Pomodoro e Basilico

Tomato and Basil Bruschetta

Technically speaking, bruschetta is just plain grilled (broiled) bread, rubbed with garlic while it is hot and then drizzled with good-quality olive oil. Use slightly stale bread that is dense enough to stop the olive oil seeping through.

4 large slices of 'country-style' bread, such as ciabatta
1 garlic clove
drizzle of extra virgin olive oil

4 ripe tomatoes
1 tablespoon shredded basil

Grill (broil), chargrill or toast the bread until it is crisp. Cut the garlic clove in half and rub the cut edge over both sides of each bread slice. Drizzle a little extra virgin olive oil over each bread slice.

Roughly chop the tomatoes and mix with the basil. Season well and pile onto the bruschetta.

PICTURE ON OPPOSITE PAGE

SERVES 4

Bruschetta al Funghi

Wild Mushroom Bruschetta

4 large slices of 'country-style' bread, such as ciabatta
1 garlic clove
drizzle of extra virgin olive oil
2 tablespoons olive oil

400 g (14 oz) selection of wild mushrooms, particularly fresh porcini, sliced if large, or chestnut mushrooms
2 garlic cloves, crushed
1 heaped tablespoon chopped thyme

Grill (broil), chargrill or toast the bread until it is crisp. Cut the garlic clove in half and rub the cut edge over both sides of each bread slice. Drizzle a little extra virgin olive oil over each bread slice.

Heat the olive oil in a large frying pan over high heat. Add just enough mushrooms to cover the base of the pan and cook, stirring frequently,

until the mushrooms are tender and any liquid has evaporated. Season with salt and pepper.

Add a little crushed garlic and thyme and cook for a further minute. Remove from the pan and repeat with the remaining mushrooms. Spoon over the bruschetta and serve immediately.

PICTURE ON OPPOSITE PAGE

SERVES 4

PANZANELLA
Bread Salad

1 garlic clove, cut in half
1 loaf 'country-style' bread, such as ciabatta
6 ripe tomatoes
1 small yellow capsicum (pepper)
½ cucumber, peeled

½ white salad onion
2 tablespoons shredded basil leaves
80 ml (3 fl oz/⅓ cup) olive oil
2 tablespoons red wine vinegar

Rub the cut side of the garlic clove over the inside of a large salad bowl. Remove the crust from the bread and cut it into cubes. Put the bread cubes in the bowl and sprinkle it with enough cold water to moisten.

Cut the tomatoes, capsicum and cucumber into chunks and dice the onion. Add the vegetables to the bread with the basil and then sprinkle with the olive oil and vinegar. Toss well and leave for 30 minutes before serving.

SERVES 4

MINESTRA DI FARRO
Spelt Soup

200 g (7 oz) dried borlotti beans
2 tablespoons olive oil
1 small onion, thinly sliced
2 garlic cloves, crushed
1.5 litres (52 fl oz/6 cups) chicken stock

8 mint leaves, roughly torn
200 g (7 oz) farro (spelt)
100 g (4 oz/1 cup) grated Parmesan cheese
1 tablespoon finely chopped mint
4 teaspoons extra virgin olive oil

Soak the borlotti beans in cold water overnight. Drain and place in a large saucepan with plenty of cold water. Bring to the boil and simmer until the beans are tender (about 1½ hours, depending on the age of the beans). Drain.

Heat the olive oil in a large saucepan and cook the onion over low heat for 6 minutes, or until soft. Season. Add the garlic and cook without browning for 20–30 seconds. Add the stock and torn mint and bring to the boil.

Stir in the farro a little at a time so that the stock continues to boil, then lower the heat and simmer for 15 minutes. Add the borlotti beans and simmer for 30 minutes, or until the farro is tender and the soup thick. Purée half the soup, then return all of the soup to the pan and stir in the grated Parmesan and the chopped mint. Season and stir in up to 250 ml (9 fl oz/1 cup) hot water to give the soup a spoonable consistency. Serve immediately, with 1 teaspoon of extra virgin olive oil stirred through each bowl.

SERVES 4

PEPERONI RIPIENI

Stuffed Capsicums

Stuffed vegetables are of Arabian origin, although they have now become almost synonymous with Mediterranean cooking. In Italy, you will find vegetables stuffed with all manner of ingredients, from rice and breadcrumbs to cheese or meat.

3 red or yellow capsicums (peppers), halved and seeded
1 tablespoon olive oil
1 small onion, finely chopped
2 garlic cloves, crushed
50 g (2 oz) butter
180 g (7 oz/2¼ cups) fresh breadcrumbs

1 egg
35 g (1 oz/⅓ cup) grated Parmesan cheese
2 tomatoes, peeled, seeded and chopped
150 g (6 oz/1 cup) grated mozzarella cheese
2 tablespoons chopped basil
3 tablespoons extra virgin olive oil

Preheat the oven to 170°C (325°F/Gas 3). Place the capsicums on a lightly oiled baking tray.

Heat the olive oil in a frying pan and cook the onion and garlic, stirring, for 5 minutes. Remove from the heat. Stir in the butter and breadcrumbs.

Transfer to a bowl and add the egg, Parmesan, tomato, mozzarella, basil and 3 tablespoons water. Stir well and season. Fill the capsicums with the stuffing, drizzle with the extra virgin olive oil and bake for 40–45 minutes, or until the capsicums are cooked through and the tops are golden brown.

PICTURE ON PAGE 22

SERVES 6

CIPOLLE RIPIENE

Stuffed Onions

8 medium white or red onions, peeled but left whole
1 tablespoon olive oil
15 g (½ oz) butter
1 onion, finely chopped
1 garlic clove, crushed

3 tomatoes, peeled, seeded and chopped
250 g (9 oz) minced (ground) beef
2 tablespoons chopped flat-leaf (Italian) parsley
1 egg
35 g (1 oz/⅓ cup) grated Parmesan cheese

Place the onions in a large saucepan, cover with water and simmer for 10 minutes. Drain and cool. Cut off the tops and scoop out some of the inside.

Preheat the oven to 180°C (350°F/Gas 4). Heat the oil and butter in a frying pan. Add the onion

and garlic and cook, stirring, for 5 minutes, or until tender. Add the tomato and cook for 6 minutes over low heat. Add the beef and cook until lightly browned. Set aside to cool. Add the parsley, egg and Parmesan and stir well. Stuff the filling into the onions and bake for 20 minutes.

PICTURE ON PAGE 22

SERVES 4

Stuffed Capsicums and Stuffed Onions (recipes on page 21)

MINESTRONE ALLA GENOVESE

Genoese Minestrone

Just about every region of Italy has its own minestrone. This version has a spoonful of pesto stirred through at the end; others have rice instead of pasta. For minestrone alla milanese, simply add 200 grams (7 ounces) of arborio rice instead of the pasta.

225 g (8 oz) dried borlotti beans
50 g (2 oz) lard or butter
1 large onion, finely chopped
1 garlic clove, finely chopped
15 g (½ oz) flat-leaf (Italian) parsley, finely chopped
2 sage leaves
100 g (4 oz) pancetta, cubed
2 celery stalks, halved then sliced
2 carrots, sliced
3 potatoes, peeled but left whole
1 teaspoon tomato paste (concentrated purée)

400 g (14 oz) tin chopped tomatoes
8 basil leaves
3 litres (105 fl oz/12 cups) chicken or vegetable stock
2 zucchini (courgettes), sliced
220 g (8 oz) shelled peas
120 g (4 oz) runner beans, cut into 4 cm (1½ in) lengths
¼ cabbage, shredded
150 g (6 oz) ditalini, avemarie or other small pasta
1 quantity pesto (page 248)
grated Parmesan cheese

Put the dried beans in a large bowl, cover with cold water and leave to soak overnight. Drain and rinse under cold water.

To make the soffritto, melt the lard in a large saucepan. Cook the onion, garlic, parsley, sage and pancetta over low heat, stirring once or twice, for 10 minutes, or until the onion is soft and golden.

Add the celery, carrot and potatoes and cook for 5 minutes. Stir in the tomato paste, tomatoes, basil and borlotti beans. Season with plenty of pepper. Add the stock and bring slowly to the boil. Cover and simmer for 2 hours, stirring once or twice.

If the potatoes haven't broken up, roughly break them up with a fork against the side of the pan. Taste for seasoning and add the zucchini, peas, runner beans, cabbage and pasta. Simmer until the pasta is al dente. Serve with a dollop of pesto and the Parmesan.

SERVES 6

Far left: Use either fresh shelled peas or frozen peas.

Left: Add the vegetables to the soffritto and cook briefly before adding the tomatoes and borlotti beans.

Frittata ai Carciofi

Artichoke Frittata

Almost an omelette, but flashed under the grill (broiler) to finish cooking, the frittata varies from thin and pancake-like, to thicker, with a golden crust and creamy centre.

175 g (6 oz) broad beans, fresh or frozen
400 g (14 oz) tin artichoke hearts, drained
3 tablespoons olive oil
1 onion, halved and thinly sliced

6 eggs
2 tablespoons chopped flat-leaf (Italian) parsley
45 g (1 ½ oz/½ cup) grated pecorino cheese
pinch of nutmeg

Bring a small saucepan of water to the boil and add a large pinch of salt and the broad beans. Boil for 2 minutes, then drain and rinse under cold water. Peel off the skins from the beans.

Cut the artichoke hearts from bottom to top into slices about 5 mm (¼ in) wide. Discard any slices that contain the tough central choke.

Heat the oil in a 30 cm (12 in) frying pan and fry the onion over low heat for 6–8 minutes, without allowing it to brown. Add the artichoke slices and cook for 1–2 minutes. Stir in the broad beans.

Preheat the grill (broiler). Lightly beat together the eggs, parsley, pecorino and nutmeg and season well with salt and pepper. Pour into the frying pan and cook over low heat until three-quarters set, shaking the pan often to stop the frittata sticking. Finish the top off under the grill and leave to cool before serving the frittata in wedges.

PICTURE ON OPPOSITE PAGE   SERVES 4

Frittata con Peperoni Rossi e Zucchine

Red Capsicum and Zucchini Frittata

1 red capsicum (pepper), sliced
2 zucchini (courgettes), sliced
1 tablespoon olive oil
1 onion, sliced

6 eggs
1 tablespoon chopped basil
50 g (2 oz/½ cup) grated Parmesan cheese

Cut the capsicum and zucchini into thin slices. Heat the olive oil in a 30 cm (12 in) frying pan and cook the onion slices until soft. Add the capsicum and zucchini and cook until soft. Preheat the grill (broiler).

Lightly beat the eggs, basil and Parmesan and season. Pour into the pan and cook over low heat until three-quarters set, shaking the pan to stop the frittata sticking. Finish the top off under the grill and leave to cool before serving in wedges.

PICTURE ON OPPOSITE PAGE   SERVES 4

SALUMI

Salumi is the term used to refer to all Italy's cured or preserved pork products, from salami and salsicce (sausages) to cured hams such as Parma, cooked hams such as prosciutto cotto, and ingredients from lard to pancetta and coppa.

Curing meat was once the only way in which meat could be enjoyed year round. A family would keep a pig to be butchered in the winter, then turn it into salumi to be eaten throughout the year. Though beef, wild boar and venison are used for making cured meats, pork has always predominated, made popular by the fact that every scrap of the animal can be used. When the pig was butchered, the fat would be rendered into lard, the best meat turned into hams and pancetta, the rest of the pig used to make salami and sausages, and the bones saved for stock. The meats would then be cured, usually by drying, smoking or preserving in fat. In Italy, you can still buy just about every part of the pig, including guanciale, cured pig's cheek; trotters, boned and stuffed to make zampone; and the neck, cured and made into coppa.

Norcia in Umbria is renowned for its pork butchers and the town gives its name to norcini, which is a term used throughout Italy to mean pork butchers. Norcini from this area traditionally travelled all over Italy during the butchering and curing season in November to ply their trade, returning home in April. Butcher shops in central Italy that specialize in local cured pork and wild boar products are known as norcineria.

In Italy, butchers display their salami marked as pork (suino) or beef (bovino), and some may be labelled salsicce rather than salami. A salami can be sold under its own name or marked 'nostrano', meaning that it is from the area or home-made. Salami change in flavour and texture according to where they are made. The Northeast tends towards heavier, more Austrian-tasting salami, the Centre prefers a more refined texture, while in the South salami are often spicy. Flavourings may also be added to standard salami – in Tuscany this is often fennel seed and in Umbria truffles are used. The larger the salami, the thinner it should be sliced.

Prosciutto crudo is a cured ham made from an air-dried pig's leg and sliced paper-thin for antipasto. Parma ham is just one type of prosciutto and many regions produce their own hams. Prosciutto salato, salted hams, are cured heavily with salt. Tuscan ham is one of the finest and these robust hams can be excellent eaten with unsalted bread. Parma and San Daniele hams are both prosciutto dolce, sweet hams, whose subtle curing and longer hanging give them a sweet, refined flavour.

Pappa al Pomodoro
Bread and Tomato Soup

Pappa al pomodoro is a Tuscan soup made, as so many great Italian dishes are, to use up leftovers – in this case bread and tomatoes. Pappa means 'mush' and that is the soup's consistency. Pappa al pomodoro is a variety of pancotto, bread soup.

2 tablespoons olive oil
3 garlic cloves, crushed
1 white onion, finely chopped
900 g (2 lb) ripe tomatoes, peeled and
  finely chopped

200 g (7 oz) stale 'country-style' bread, such as ciabatta,
  thickly sliced and crusts removed, broken into pieces
850 ml (30 fl oz/3⅓ cups) hot chicken stock
20 basil leaves, shredded
drizzle of extra virgin olive oil

Heat the oil in a large saucepan. Cook the garlic and onion over low heat for 6–8 minutes, or until soft but not browned. Add the tomatoes. Season. Cover and simmer for 30 minutes. Add the bread and simmer, stirring once or twice, for 5 minutes.

Gradually stir in the stock. Cook, stirring, until the bread has broken down and the soup is thick. Remove from the heat and add the basil. Cover and leave for 1 hour. Serve at room temperature or reheat. Serve drizzled with extra virgin olive.

PICTURE ON OPPOSITE PAGE

SERVES 4

Funghi Ripieni
Stuffed Mushrooms

8 large flat mushrooms, stalks removed
1½ tablespoons lemon juice
12 button mushrooms, finely chopped
1 tablespoon butter
1 French shallot, finely chopped
1 garlic clove, crushed
2 tablespoons white wine

100 g (4 oz/1 cup) grated Parmesan cheese,
  plus 1 tablespoon to serve
55 g (2 oz/⅔ cup) fresh breadcrumbs
1 egg, lightly beaten
3 tablespoons thick (double/heavy) cream
1 tablespoon chopped tarragon
1 tablespoon chopped flat-leaf (Italian) parsley

Preheat the oven to 150°C (300°F/Gas 2). Rub the whole mushrooms with a little lemon juice. Mix the chopped mushrooms with the remaining juice.

Heat the butter in a small frying pan and cook the shallot and garlic for 4 minutes. Add the wine

and chopped mushrooms and cook for 4 minutes. Remove from the heat and stir in the Parmesan, breadcrumbs, egg, cream and tarragon. Season. Place the mushroom caps on a lightly oiled baking tray and stuff with the filling. Bake for 12 minutes. Sprinkle with the Parmesan and parsley and serve.

SERVES 4

SUPPLÌ

Fried Rice Balls

When these croquettes are bitten into, the mozzarella pulls out to resemble strands of telephone wires, hence the Italian name for this dish, supplì al telefono. Supplì are excellent for using up leftover risotto.

3 tablespoons butter
1 small onion, finely chopped
1.5 litres (52 fl oz/6 cups) chicken stock
440 g (16 oz/2 cups) risotto rice (arborio, vialone nano
    or carnaroli)
75 g (3 oz/¾ cup) grated Parmesan cheese

2 eggs, beaten
9 basil leaves, torn in half
150 g (6 oz) mozzarella cheese, cut into 18 cubes
    about 1.5 cm (⅝ in) square
150 g (6 oz/1½ cups) dried breadcrumbs
oil, for deep-frying

Melt the butter in a large saucepan. Add the onion and cook over low heat for 3–4 minutes, or until soft but not browned. Heat the stock to simmering point in another saucepan.

Add the rice to the onion and cook, stirring, for 1 minute to seal the rice. Add several ladles of the hot stock, stirring constantly so that the rice cooks evenly. Keep adding enough stock to just cover the rice, stirring frequently. Continue in this way for about 20 minutes, or until the rice is creamy on the outside but still al dente.

Remove from the heat and stir in the Parmesan and eggs. Season with salt and pepper. Spread out the rice on a large baking tray to cool completely.

Divide the rice into 18 portions. Take one portion in the palm of your hand and place a piece of basil and a cube of mozzarella in the centre. Fold the rice over to encase the cheese and at the same time mould the croquette into an egg shape. Roll the croquette in breadcrumbs and place on a baking tray while you make the rest.

Heat enough oil in a deep-fat fryer or deep frying pan to fully cover the croquettes. Heat the oil to 180°C (350°F), or until a piece of bread fries golden brown in 15 seconds when dropped in the oil. Deep-fry the supplì in batches, without crowding, for about 4 minutes, or until evenly golden brown. Drain on paper towels and serve at once, as they are or with a fresh tomato sauce (page 244).

SERVES 6

Right: Shaping the supplì takes a little practice but, if the rice is the right consistency, it is fairly easy.

Far right: Make sure the basil and mozzarella filling is fully enclosed so it doesn't spill out when the supplì are fried.

CARPACCIO

Sliced Raw Beef

Carpaccio is named after the Renaissance painter whose use of reds is reflected in the dish. It was created in Harry's Bar in Venice for a favourite customer whose doctor had placed her on a diet forbidding cooked meat.

700 g (1 lb 9 oz) good-quality beef fillet
1 egg yolk
3 teaspoons dijon mustard
3 tablespoons lemon juice

2 drops Tabasco sauce
80 ml (3 fl oz/⅓ cup) olive oil
1 tablespoon cream
2–3 tablespoons capers, rinsed

Place the beef in the freezer for about half an hour, or until it is firm. Using a sharp knife or mandolin, cut the beef into paper-thin slices. Arrange on six serving plates in an even layer.

Blend together the egg yolk, mustard, lemon juice and Tabasco in a bowl or food processor. Add the

olive oil in a thin stream, whisking or processing constantly until the mayonnaise thickens. Whisk in the cream. Season to taste with salt and pepper. Drizzle the mayonnaise over the beef slices and sprinkle with the capers.

PICTURE ON OPPOSITE PAGE

SERVES 6

ASPARAGI ALLA BRACE

Chargrilled Asparagus

24 asparagus spears
1 tablespoon extra virgin olive oil

2 tablespoons balsamic vinegar
Parmesan cheese shavings

Wash the asparagus and remove the woody ends (hold each spear at both ends and bend gently – it will snap at its natural breaking point).

Put the asparagus in a bowl, add the olive oil and toss well. Heat a chargrill pan (griddle) or barbecue and cook the asparagus for about 10 minutes, or

until al dente. Drizzle with balsamic vinegar and sprinkle with the Parmesan shavings to serve.

(If you don't have a chargrill pan or barbecue, you can steam the asparagus or boil in salted water for 6–8 minutes until al dente. Drain and mix with the olive oil, balsamic and Parmesan.)

SERVES 4

La Ribollita

Tuscan Bean Soup

Ribollita means 'reboiled' because this Tuscan bean soup is best made a day in advance to let the flavours develop, then reheated. It should then be thick enough to eat with a fork rather than a spoon.

4 tablespoons olive oil
1 onion, finely chopped
1 large carrot, finely chopped
3 celery stalks, finely chopped
2 large garlic cloves, crushed
250 g (9 oz) cavolo nero or savoy cabbage
1 zucchini (courgette), finely chopped
400 g (14 oz) cooked cannellini or borlotti beans

400 g (14 oz) tin tomatoes
185 ml (6 fl oz/$^3/_4$ cup) red wine
1 litre (35 fl oz/4 cups) chicken stock or water
75 g (3 oz) stale 'country-style' bread, such as
    ciabatta or pugliese, crusts removed and broken
    into 2.5 cm (1 in) cubes
drizzle of extra virgin olive oil

To make the soffritto, pour the olive oil into a large saucepan and add the onion. Cook the onion gently – use this time to chop the carrot and celery and add them to the pan as you go along. Once you have added the garlic, cook for a few minutes.

Strip the leaves of the cavolo from the stems or cut away the thick stem of the savoy. Wash and finely chop the stems and roughly chop the leaves. Add the cabbage stems and the zucchini to the soffritto and cook, stirring occasionally, for about 5 minutes, or until the vegetables have changed to an opaque colour and soaked up some of the olive oil.

Stir in the beans and cook for 5 minutes more, then add the tomatoes and cook for a further 5 minutes to reduce the liquid.

Add the cabbage leaves and mix into the soup, stirring until just wilted. Add the wine and stock or water and gently simmer for about 40 minutes.

Add the bread to the pan (if the bread is very fresh, dry it out a little in the oven first to prevent it disintegrating into the soup). Mix briefly and remove the pan from the heat. Leave for about 30 minutes. This rests the soup and allows the flavours to mingle. Serve it hot but not boiling, with a generous drizzle of extra virgin olive oil.

If reheating the soup, make sure it comes to the boil but then remove it from the heat and leave to cool for 5 minutes. Serve in cold bowls. The soup should be warm, rather than piping hot.

SERVES 4

Food Journey

CHEESE

As well as making famous cheeses like Parmigiano Reggiano or mozzarella, Italian cheesemakers create hundreds of regional cheeses, fresh and aged, and many are never found outside Italy.

The history of cheese in Italy is very closely related to the country's varied geography. The rich mountainous pastures of the North produce hundreds of cheeses like fontina, Gorgonzola, mascarpone, Asiago, Grana Padano and Taleggio. In the Centre, Emilia-Romagna is the home of Parmigiano Reggiano (Parmesan), perhaps Italy's most famous cheese. Tuscany and Umbria produce fresh pecorinos, while the sparser and hotter South is more suited to farming sheep and goats than cows. These sheep and goat's cheeses are usually harder than the French chèvre and are suitable for grating, though you can also find soft, fresh cheeses like sheep's ricotta. The South is also the home of pasta filata, cheeses made from stretched out curds like mozzarella and provolone. In Campania, buffalo milk is used to make mozzarella.

Many of the traditional methods for making cheese are safeguarded by consorzi (cooperatives), who have imposed their own rules for production to ensure their cheeses are made to the highest quality, using the best milk in each area. The rules for production can include methods passed down through centuries, such as milking Parmesan cows by hand, and this explains the often higher cost of these cheeses. Cheeses from these cooperatives are usually awarded a DOC (Denominazione di Origine Controllata) rating in the form of a brand or stamp on the rind.

Italian cheeses can be made from cow's, buffalo's, goat's and sheep's milk. Cow's milk is used more in the North, while buffaloes are farmed around Naples and almost all of the milk is used to make mozzarella di bufala. Goat's and sheep's cheeses are increasingly popular. Most are produced in Tuscany, Umbria and the South. Both pasteurized and unpasteurized cheeses are made in Italy, with unpasteurized or partly unpasteurized cheeses, such as caciocavallo and provolone, continuing to develop as they age.

Italian cheeses are also divided into hard and soft cheeses. Hard cheeses have a water content of less than 40 per cent and include those cheeses used for cooking like Grana Padano and pecorino. Soft cheeses have a water content of more than 40 per cent and are best eaten as soon as possible after being made. They include cheeses such as mascarpone and mozzarella, which should be eaten the day they are made.

Unlike French cheeses, Italian cheeses are more famous for their use in cooking than for being eaten as a separate cheese course. In Italy though, cheeses are often eaten at every course, in cooking and as table cheeses. Cooking cheeses are known as formaggio per cucina and perhaps the most famous is Parmigiano Reggiano, rarely eaten as part of a cheese platter outside of Italy. Table cheeses are known as formaggio da tavola. Both fresh and hard cheeses are eaten on their own.

Taleggio
Cademartori
£ 2500 hg

Arancini

Fried Rice Balls with Thyme

Arancini – the name means 'little oranges' – are a speciality of Sicily. The saffron risotto is traditional. If you can find it, use vialone nano or another semi-fine rice – the glutinous texture keeps the grains of rice together.

large pinch of saffron threads
250 ml (9 fl oz/1 cup) white wine
100 g (4 oz) butter
1 onion, finely chopped
1 large garlic clove, crushed
750 ml (27 fl oz/3 cups) chicken stock
2 tablespoons thyme

220 g (8 oz/1 cup) risotto rice (arborio, vialone nano or carnaroli)
50 g (2 oz/1/2 cup) grated Parmesan cheese
100 g (4 oz) mozzarella or fontina cheese, cut into cubes
75 g (3 oz/3/4 cup) dried breadcrumbs
oil, for deep-frying

Leave the saffron to soak in the wine while you prepare the risotto. Melt the butter in a large saucepan. Add the onion and garlic and cook over low heat for 3–4 minutes, or until softened but not browned. Heat the stock to simmering point in another saucepan.

Add the thyme and the rice to the onion and cook, stirring, for 1 minute to seal the rice. Add the wine and saffron and stir until the wine is all absorbed. Add several ladles of the hot stock, stirring constantly so that the rice cooks evenly. Keep adding enough stock to just cover the rice, stirring frequently. Continue in this way for about 20 minutes, or until the rice is creamy.

For arancini it is not so essential to keep the rice al dente. Add more water or chicken stock if the rice is not fully cooked. Make sure all this liquid is absorbed. Remove from the heat and stir in the Parmesan, then spread out onto a tray covered with plastic wrap. Leave to cool and, if possible, leave in the refrigerator overnight.

To make the arancini, roll a small amount of risotto into a walnut-sized ball. Press a hole in the middle with your thumb, place a small piece of cheese inside and press the risotto around it to enclose in a ball. Repeat with the rest of the risotto. Roll each risotto ball in the breadcrumbs, pressing down to coat well.

Heat enough oil in a deep-fat fryer or deep frying pan to cover the arancini. Heat the oil to 180°C (350°F), or until a piece of bread fries golden brown in 15 seconds when dropped in the oil. Deep-fry the arancini in batches for 3–4 minutes. Drain on paper towels and leave for a couple of minutes before eating. Serve the arancini hot or at room temperature.

MAKES 20

Bagna Caoda

Garlic and Anchovy Dip

185 ml (6 fl oz/¾ cup) olive oil
6 garlic cloves, crushed
120 g (4 oz) anchovy fillets, finely minced
90 g (3 oz) butter

40 pieces assorted raw vegetables (carrot, celery, fennel
  or cauliflower florets), cut into strips for dipping
'country-style' bread, such as ciabatta

Gently cook the oil, garlic and anchovies in a saucepan over moderately low heat, stirring once or twice, until the anchovies dissolve. Do not let the garlic brown. Add the butter and leave over low heat until it has melted. Season with pepper.

Transfer the sauce to a bowl and keep warm at the table by placing on a food warmer or over a burner or spirit stove. Serve the vegetables and bread on a platter. Guests dip their choice of vegetable into the sauce and use the bread to catch any drips.

SERVES 4

Caponata

Sicilian Vegetables

1 kg (2 lb 4 oz) eggplants (aubergines), cut into 2 cm
  (¾ in) cubes
½ tablespoon salt
250 ml (9 fl oz/1 cup) olive oil
1 large onion, roughly chopped
2 celery stalks, sliced
1 small red capsicum (pepper), cut into short strips

2 tablespoons pine nuts
400 g (14 oz) tin chopped tomatoes
4 tablespoons red wine vinegar
1 tablespoon sugar
2 tablespoons capers, rinsed and chopped if large
24 green olives, pitted and halved
4 tablespoons finely chopped flat-leaf (Italian) parsley

Layer the eggplant cubes in a colander, sprinkling each layer with salt as you go. Leave to drain for 30 minutes. Rinse and squeeze the eggplant dry. Heat 4 tablespoons of the oil in a large frying pan. Brown the eggplant in batches over high heat, adding oil as needed. Drain on paper towels.

Add more oil to the pan, reduce the heat and cook the onion and celery for 5 minutes, or until soft but not brown. Add the red capsicum and pine nuts and cook for 2 minutes. Spoon off any excess oil and add the tomatoes and 3 tablespoons water. Simmer for 10 minutes, or until the mixture is quite dry. Season well with black pepper.

Add the vinegar, sugar, capers and olives and cook over low heat for 2–3 minutes. Add the eggplant, cook for 5–6 minutes, then remove from the heat and leave to cool. Taste for pepper and stir in the parsley to serve.

SERVES 6

ZUPPA DI PESCE

Fish Soup

For a country where almost every region has a sea coast, it is hardly surprising that Italy has almost as many versions of this soup as there are fish in the sea. This recipe includes suggestions for fish to use, but ask your fishmonger what's best on the day.

FISH STOCK
300 g (11 oz) firm white fish fillets, such as monkfish, red mullet, cod, deep sea perch, skinned and cut into large cubes, bones reserved
12 prawns (shrimp)
1 small onion, roughly chopped
1 carrot, roughly chopped
15 g (½ oz) flat-leaf (Italian) parsley, roughly chopped, stalks reserved

200 g (7 oz) squid tubes
4 tablespoons olive oil
1 onion, finely chopped

1 celery stalk, finely chopped
1 carrot, finely chopped
2 garlic cloves, finely chopped
pinch of cayenne pepper
1 fennel bulb, trimmed and thinly sliced
125 ml (4 fl oz/½ cup) dry white wine
400 g (14 oz) tin chopped tomatoes
250 g (9 oz) scallops, cleaned

CROSTINI
3 tablespoons extra virgin olive oil
2 garlic cloves, crushed
4 slices 'country-style' bread, such as ciabatta

To make the fish stock, rinse the fish bones in cold water, removing any blood or intestines. Peel and devein the prawns and put the fish bones and prawn shells in a large saucepan with just enough water to cover. Bring slowly to a simmer, skimming any froth from the surface. Add the onion, carrot and stalks from the parsley, then simmer gently for 20 minutes. Strain through a fine colander and measure 1.5 litres (52 fl oz/6 cups) stock. If there is less stock than this, add a little water; if there is more stock than this, put the strained stock back into the saucepan and simmer until reduced to 1.5 litres (52 fl oz/6 cups).

Lie the squid out flat, skin side up, and score a crisscross pattern into the flesh, being careful not to cut all the way through. Slice diagonally into bite-sized strips.

Heat the oil in a large saucepan and cook the onion, celery, carrot, garlic and chopped parsley over moderately low heat for 5–6 minutes, or until soft but not browned. Add the cayenne pepper and season. Stir in the fennel and cook for 2–3 minutes. Add the white wine, increase the heat and cook until it has been absorbed. Stir in the tomatoes, then add the fish stock and bring to the boil. Reduce the heat and simmer for 20 minutes.

Add the squid to the pan with the fish pieces and simmer for 1 minute. Add the scallops and prawns and simmer for a further 2 minutes. Taste and add more seasoning if necessary.

To make the crostini, heat the olive oil and garlic in a large frying pan over moderately low heat. Add the slices of bread and fry on both sides until golden. Place a slice of bread into each of four warmed serving bowls. Ladle the soup on top and serve immediately.

PICTURE ON PAGE 50

SERVES 4

Fish Soup (recipe on page 49)

Acciughe Marinate

Marinated Fresh Anchovies

Anchovies are fished all over the Mediterranean, as well as the Atlantic coasts of France and Spain. You will need very fresh fish for this simple dish, with perhaps just some bread to mop up juices. The dish can be kept refrigerated for up to three days.

400 g (14 oz) fresh anchovies
60 ml (2 fl oz/¼ cup) olive oil
1 tablespoon extra virgin olive oil
3 tablespoons lemon juice

2 garlic cloves, crushed
2 tablespoons finely chopped flat-leaf (Italian) parsley
2 tablespoons finely chopped basil
1 small red chilli, seeded and chopped

Fillet the anchovies by running a sharp knife along the backbone, then pulling the head upwards. The head, bones and guts should all come away, leaving the fillets. Rinse and pat dry with paper towels.

Mix the remaining ingredients together with some salt and pepper and pour over the anchovies in a shallow serving bowl. Cover with plastic wrap and marinate in the refrigerator for at least 3 hours.

PICTURE ON OPPOSITE PAGE

SERVES 4

Polpo alla Brace

Chargrilled Octopus

Buy small octopus if you can find them – they are more tender than the large ones. If only large are available, tenderize them by beating with a rolling pin before cooking. In some coastal regions, you can see octopus being tenderized in a cement mixer.

16 small octopus (about 1.5 kg/3 lb 5 oz)
170 ml (6 fl oz/⅔ cup) extra virgin olive oil
4 sprigs of thyme

2 bay leaves
2 garlic cloves, crushed
lemon wedges

Clean the octopus by slitting the head and pulling out the innards. Cut out the eyes and beak and rinse. Skin the tentacles and make small diagonal cuts along their length, cutting a third of the way through. Place in a bowl and pour over the oil. Add the thyme, bay leaves and garlic and toss well. Marinate overnight in the refrigerator. Soak four wooden skewers in water.

Heat the chargrill pan (griddle) or a barbecue. Drain the excess oil from the octopus and thread onto the skewers. Cook for 5–7 minutes on each side or until the octopus is golden and the tip of a knife slips through a tentacle. Season with salt and pepper and drizzle with some extra marinade or extra virgin olive oil if you like. Leave for a few minutes and then serve with lemon wedges.

SERVES 4

Insalata Caprese

Tomato, Mozzarella and Basil Salad

Insalata caprese is traditionally served with no other dressing than a drizzle of extra virgin olive oil. However, if you're not absolutely confident that your tomatoes have the best flavour, a little balsamic vinegar will help them along.

6 ripe Roma (plum) tomatoes
3–4 balls mozzarella cheese
2 tablespoons extra virgin olive oil

15 young basil leaves
½ teaspoon balsamic vinegar (optional)

Slice the tomatoes, pouring off any excess juice, and cut the mozzarella cheese into slices of a similar thickness. Arrange alternating rows of the tomato and mozzarella slices on a serving plate. Sprinkle with salt and pepper.

Drizzle the extra virgin olive oil over the tomato and mozzarella. Tear the basil into pieces and scatter over the oil. To serve, take to the table and sprinkle the salad with the balsamic vinegar, if you're using it.

PICTURE ON OPPOSITE PAGE

SERVES 4

Insalata di Carciofi

Artichokes Vinaigrette

Only small young artichokes of a few varieties, such as Violetto Toscano, are tender enough to be eaten raw. If they are unavailable, use cooked hearts, either fresh or tinned. Allow one heart per person as part of an antipasto, two each as a first course.

2 tablespoons lemon juice
4 young Romanesco or Violetto Toscano artichokes

1 quantity vinaigrette (page 249)

Mix the lemon juice in a large bowl with 1 litre (35 fl oz/4 cups) cold water. Using kitchen scissors or a sharp knife, cut off and discard the top third of each artichoke and all the tough outer leaves. Snip off any spikes on the remaining leaves. Chop off and discard all but 2–3 cm (¾–1¼ in) of the stem and peel this with a potato peeler. Slice each artichoke in half from top to bottom, including the stem. Scrape out the furry choke and discard it. As each artichoke is prepared, place it straight into the bowl of lemon water to avoid discolouring.

Shake each artichoke half dry and arrange on a serving platter. Spoon the vinaigrette over the top and leave for at least 30 minutes before serving.

SERVES 4

Chapter 2

SEAFOOD

Each region of Italy has its signature fish and seafood dishes, particularly stews. Dishes are largely simply prepared, allowing the distinctive flavour of the fish to shine through. Salt cod is often sold pre-soaked, ready for use.

Cozze Ripiene

Stuffed Mussels

Mussels are especially popular in the Puglia region – the heel of Italy's 'boot'. This dish, flavoured with olive oil, garlic, tomato and basil, epitomizes the flavours of that stretch of Mediterranean coast.

24 mussels
3 tablespoons olive oil
4 garlic cloves, crushed
500 ml (17 fl oz/2 cups) tomato passata
1½ tablespoons roughly chopped basil

15 g (½ oz/¼ cup) finely chopped flat-leaf
  (Italian) parsley
40 g (1½ oz/½ cup) fresh white breadcrumbs
2 eggs, beaten
pinch of cayenne pepper

Clean the mussels by scrubbing them thoroughly. Discard any that are broken or cracked or do not close when tapped on the work surface. Insert a sharp knife at the point where the beard protrudes and prise the shell open, leaving the mussel intact inside and keeping the two shells attached. Pull out the beard and discard. Rinse the mussels.

Heat the olive oil in a large saucepan and gently cook half the garlic for 15–20 seconds, without browning. Add the passata and basil, season lightly and bring to the boil. Reduce the heat and simmer for 5 minutes, then add 310 ml (11 fl oz/1¼ cups) cold water. Return to the boil, cover and keep at a low simmer.

Combine the parsley, breadcrumbs and remaining garlic, then blend in the eggs. Add the cayenne pepper and season the mixture. Using a teaspoon, fill each mussel with a little of this mixture. Tie the mussels closed with kitchen string as you go, to prevent the filling escaping.

When all the mussels have been stuffed, place them in the tomato sauce and simmer, covered, for 10 minutes. Lift out with a slotted spoon and remove the string. Pile on a warm platter and serve with the tomato sauce, bread and finger bowls.

SERVES 4

Far left: Large mussels will be easier to fill than smaller ones.

Left: Tie the stuffed mussels with kitchen string to prevent the filling from escaping. Remember to remove the string before serving the mussels.

Tonno con Fagioli
Tuna with Beans

400 g (14 oz) dried beans, such as cannellini
1 bay leaf
1 garlic clove
125 ml (4 fl oz/½ cup) olive oil

1 small red onion, thinly sliced
2 tablespoons finely chopped flat-leaf (Italian) parsley
400 g (14 oz) tin tuna in olive oil, drained

Soak the beans overnight in plenty of cold water. Rinse them and transfer to a very large saucepan. Cover with plenty of cold water and bring to the boil. Add the bay leaf, garlic and 1 tablespoon olive oil, cover and simmer for 1–1½ hours, or until tender. Salt the water for the last 15–20 minutes of cooking. The beans should keep their shape and have a slight bite rather than being soft.

Drain well, discard the bay leaf and garlic and transfer the beans to a shallow serving dish. Add the onion and remaining oil and season. Toss well, then chill.

Toss through two-thirds of the parsley. Break the tuna into pieces and toss through the beans. Serve sprinkled with the remaining parsley.

PICTURE ON OPPOSITE PAGE

SERVES 4

Triglie al Finocchio
Red Mullet with Fennel

2 fennel bulbs
2 tablespoons butter
2 tablespoons olive oil
1 onion, chopped
1 garlic clove, crushed

4 red mullet, gutted and scaled
extra virgin olive oil
1 lemon, quartered
2 teaspoons chopped oregano
lemon wedges

Preheat the oven to 190°C (375°F/Gas 5) and grease a large shallow ovenproof dish. Finely slice the fennel, keeping the green fronds.

Heat the butter and olive oil in a large frying pan and gently cook the fennel, onion and garlic for 12–15 minutes, until softened but not browned. Season with salt and pepper. Stuff each fish with a heaped tablespoon of the fennel mixture and a quarter of the fennel fronds.

Brush the fish with extra virgin olive oil, squeeze a lemon quarter over each and season well.

Spoon the remainder of the cooked fennel mixture into the dish and sprinkle with half of the oregano. Arrange the fish, side by side, on top. Sprinkle the remaining oregano over the fish and cover the dish loosely with foil. Bake for 25 minutes, or until just cooked through. Serve with lemon wedges.

SERVES 4

Burrida

Ligurian Fish Stew

The fish suggestions below are merely a guide. Take your fishmonger's advice on what is fresh and seasonal. Ask for the fish to be prepared and cut into large chunks, though you will need the bones for your stock (this can be made in advance and frozen).

FISH STOCK
250 g (9 oz) red mullet or red snapper fillet, cut into
  chunks, bones reserved
250 g (9 oz) cod, halibut or turbot fillet, cut into chunks,
  bones reserved
250 g (9 oz) monkfish fillet, or any other firm white fish,
  cut into chunks, bones reserved
6 large prawns (shrimp) or langoustines
1 small onion, roughly chopped
1 carrot, roughly chopped
15 g (½ oz) flat-leaf (Italian) parsley, roughly chopped,
  stalks reserved

SOUP BASE
125 ml (4 fl oz/½ cup) olive oil
1 red onion, halved and thinly sliced
1 large fennel bulb, thinly sliced
3 garlic cloves, thinly sliced
800 g (1 lb 12 oz) tin tomatoes
310 ml (11 fl oz/1¼ cups) dry white vermouth or wine
large pinch of saffron threads
450 g (1 lb) waxy potatoes, quartered lengthways
450 g (1 lb) mussels

To make the fish stock, rinse the fish bones in cold water, removing any blood or intestines. Peel and devein the prawns and put the fish bones and prawn shells in a large saucepan with just enough water to cover. Bring slowly to a simmer, skimming any froth from the surface. Add the onion, carrot and the stalks from the parsley, then simmer gently for 20 minutes. Strain through a fine colander and measure 1 litre (35 fl oz/4 cups) stock. If there is more than this, put the strained stock back into the saucepan and simmer until reduced to 1 litre (35 fl oz/4 cups).

To make the soup base, heat the olive oil in a large saucepan and cook the onion and fennel for about 5 minutes to soften. Add the garlic and tomatoes. Bring to the boil, then reduce the heat and simmer until the tomatoes have reduced to a thick sauce. Season and add 200 ml (7 fl oz) of the vermouth, the saffron and potatoes. Increase the heat and

boil for about 5 minutes, then add the fish stock, reduce the heat and simmer for 10 minutes, or until the potatoes are cooked.

Scrub the mussels, pull off the beards and discard any that are broken or cracked or don't close when tapped on the work surface. Bring the remaining vermouth to the boil in another saucepan and add the mussels. Cover and cook quickly for 1 minute, or until the shells have just opened (discard any that stay closed). Remove the mussels from their shells and place in a bowl. Pour over the remaining cooking liquid, discarding any sediment in the pan.

Add the prawns and fish to the soup. Stir briefly, season and simmer for 5 minutes, until the fish is cooked. Add the mussels at the last moment to reheat. Remove from the heat and leave for at least 10 minutes before serving. Add the parsley and serve in hot bowls with bread or crostini.

SERVES 6

Pesce Spada al Forno

Sicilian Baked Swordfish

Fished mainly off the coast of Sicily, swordfish has a firm meaty texture. While many more delicate fish would be overpowered by the strong Mediterranean flavours of this dish, the more robust flesh of the swordfish can hold its own.

80 ml (3 fl oz/⅓ cup) olive oil
2 tablespoons lemon juice
2½ tablespoons finely chopped basil
4 swordfish steaks
60 g (2 oz) pitted black olives, chopped

1 tablespoon baby capers
½ teaspoon finely chopped anchovies in olive oil
400 g (14 oz) tomatoes, peeled, seeded and chopped
2 tablespoons dried breadcrumbs

Mix half the olive oil with the lemon juice and 1 tablespoon of the basil. Season and pour into a shallow ovenproof dish, large enough to hold the swordfish in a single layer. Arrange the swordfish in the dish and leave to marinate for 15 minutes, turning once. Preheat the oven to 230°C (450°F/Gas 8) and preheat the grill (broiler).

Combine the olives, capers, anchovies and tomatoes with the remaining oil and basil and season well. Spread over the swordfish and sprinkle with the breadcrumbs. Bake for 20 minutes, or until the fish is just opaque. Finish off by placing briefly under the hot grill (broiler) until the breadcrumbs are crisp. Serve with bread to soak up the juices.

SERVES 4

Anguilla al Forno

Roast Eel with Bay Leaves

2 x 800 g (1 lb 12 oz) eels or
   1 x 1.25 kg (2 lb 12 oz) eel, skinned
2 lemons, halved

4 garlic cloves
25–30 large fresh bay leaves
coarse sea salt

Preheat the oven to 200°C (400°F/Gas 6). Lightly brush a large shallow casserole with oil.

Rub the eel with a cloth to wipe off some of the shine, then rub it with the cut side of half a lemon. Cut the eel into 5 cm (2 in) sections, discarding the head and the section that contains the gut.

Arrange half the eel pieces in a single layer in the casserole. Scatter with the garlic cloves and squeeze some lemon juice over the top. Sprinkle lightly with pepper. Scatter half the bay leaves over the top, then liberally sprinkle with salt. Repeat the layers with the remaining ingredients. Bake for 35–40 minutes, or until the eel is tender.

SERVES 4

Calamari Ripieni

Stuffed Calamari

If your fishmonger has had a catch of small tender squid, snap them up – this is the perfect recipe for them. If you are having to make do with larger squid, you might need to increase the cooking time and take care that the liquid does not evaporate.

TOMATO SAUCE
800 g (1 lb 12 oz) tin tomatoes
125 ml (4 fl oz/½ cup) red wine
2 tablespoons chopped flat-leaf (Italian) parsley
pinch of sugar

STUFFING
600 g (1 lb 5 oz) small squid
80 ml (3 fl oz/⅓ cup) olive oil

1 small onion, finely chopped
1 small fennel bulb, finely chopped
2 garlic cloves, crushed
75 g (3 oz/⅓ cup) risotto rice (arborio, vialone nano or carnaroli)
large pinch of saffron threads
½ large red chilli, chopped
170 ml (6 fl oz/⅔ cup) white wine
2 tablespoons chopped flat-leaf (Italian) parsley

To make the sauce, put the tomatoes, red wine, parsley and sugar in a saucepan. Season and simmer until some of the liquid has evaporated.

To make the stuffing, prepare the squid by pulling the heads and tentacles out of the bodies with any innards. Cut the heads off below the eyes, leaving just the tentacles. Rinse the bodies, pulling out the transparent quills. Finely chop the tentacles and set aside with the squid bodies.

Heat the oil in a saucepan, add the onion, fennel and garlic and cook gently for 10 minutes, or until soft. Add the rice, saffron, red chilli and chopped squid tentacles and cook for a few minutes, stirring frequently until the tentacles are opaque. Season and add the wine and 6 tablespoons of the tomato sauce. Cook, stirring frequently, until the wine and tomato have reduced. Add 125 ml (4 fl oz/½ cup) water and continue cooking until the rice is tender and all of the liquid has been absorbed. Add the parsley and cool for a few minutes.

Stuff the squid with the filling, using a teaspoon to push the filling down to the bottom of the squid sacks. Do not overfill – you need to close the tops of the sacks easily without any filling squeezing out. Seal the tops with cocktail sticks.

Put the remaining tomato sauce in a saucepan with 185 ml (6 fl oz/¾ cup) of water. Cook for 2 minutes, then add the squid, cover the pan and simmer gently for 30–45 minutes, depending on the size of the squid, until soft and tender. Don't stir, or the filling may fall out (if a little filling does fall out it will merely add flavour to the sauce). Shake the pan a little if you are worried about sticking.

Remove the cocktail sticks from the squid before serving, preferably with a salad and some bread.

PICTURE ON PAGE 68

SERVES 4

Stuffed Calamari (recipe on page 67)

Frutti di Mare alla Brace

Chargrilled Shellfish

This recipe calls for Dublin Bay prawns (scampi or gamberoni) but, if you can't find them, any prawns (shrimp) will do. Using a rosemary twig for basting gives the marinade a subtle herb flavour, without allowing it to become overpowering.

125 ml (4 fl oz/½ cup) extra virgin olive oil
2 garlic cloves
1 tablespoon finely chopped basil
80 ml (3 fl oz/⅓ cup) lemon juice
12 Dublin Bay prawns (scampi or gamberoni)

12 scallops in the half shell
16 prawns (shrimp)
long sturdy twig of rosemary, for basting
16 large clams (sea dates, warty venus shells,
   pipis or vongole)

Combine the oil, garlic cloves, basil and lemon juice in a bowl and season well. Set aside to infuse for 15–20 minutes.

Remove the claws and heads from the Dublin Bay prawns, then butterfly by splitting them down the underside with a knife and opening them out.

Remove the scallops from their shells, reserving the shells, and pull away the white muscle and digestive tract around each one, leaving the roes intact if you like. Peel and devein the prawns, leaving the tails intact.

Preheat a chargrill pan (griddle) or barbecue until hot. Using the rosemary twig as a brush, lightly brush the cut surfaces of the Dublin Bay prawns with the dressing. Brush the chargrill pan (griddle) or barbecue plate with the dressing (be careful of the flame flaring) and place the Dublin Bay prawns on to cook, shell sides down.

After 30 seconds, brush the scallops with the oil dressing and add them to the chargrill pan (griddle) with the prawns and clams (discard any clams that are broken or don't close when tapped). Turn the Dublin Bay prawns over and cook for 1 minute. Turn the prawns once. Baste with more dressing once or twice. All the shellfish should be ready within 3–4 minutes – the clams can be moved to the side and brushed with a little dressing as they open. Put the scallops back on their shells.

Discard the garlic cloves and pour the oil dressing into a small serving bowl. Transfer the shellfish to a warm serving platter. Serve at once with the dressing, bread and finger bowls.

SERVES 4

SARDINE RIPIENE

Stuffed Sardines

To make a sardine dish memorable the fish must be really fresh. Sardines do not last long out of the water so don't attempt this recipe if the fish look tired. This recipe will serve two as a main course or four as an antipasto.

8 medium-sized sardines, heads removed, scaled and gutted
4 tablespoons olive oil
1 small onion, thinly sliced
1 fennel bulb, thinly sliced
50 g (2 oz/⅓ cup) pine nuts

4 tablespoons flat-leaf (Italian) parsley, roughly chopped
20 g (1 oz/¼ cup) fresh breadcrumbs
1 large garlic clove, crushed
juice of ½ lemon
extra virgin olive oil
lemon wedges

Butterfly the sardines by pressing your fingers on either side of the backbone and gently easing it away from the flesh, following the line of the bone. Remove the bone, leaving the tail attached to the flesh. The fresher the fish, the harder this is to do, so you might want to ask your fishmonger to butterfly the sardines for you. (Alternatively, use fillets and put them back together to form a whole after cooking, although the result will not be as neat.) Rinse the fish and drain on paper towels. Leave in the refrigerator until needed.

Preheat the oven to 200°C (400°F/Gas 6). To prepare the stuffing, heat the olive oil in a frying pan and add the onion, fennel and pine nuts. Cook over moderately high heat until soft and light brown, stirring frequently. Mix 1 tablespoon of the parsley with 1 tablespoon of breadcrumbs and set aside. Add the garlic and the remaining breadcrumbs to the pan and cook the stuffing for a few minutes more. Add the rest of the parsley, season and set aside. (This mixture can be made in advance and kept in the refrigerator, but bring it back to room temperature before cooking.)

Drizzle a little olive oil in an ovenproof dish that will fit eight sardines in a single layer. Arrange the fish in the dish, skin side down, and season with salt and pepper. Spread the stuffing over the sardines and fold over to encase. (If you are using fillets, spread half with stuffing, then place the other fillets on top, skin-side up, tail to tail like a sandwich.) Season again and sprinkle with the parsley and breadcrumb mixture. Drizzle with the lemon juice and a little extra virgin olive oil.

Bake for 5–10 minutes, depending on the size of the sardines. (If the filling is still warm the sardines will cook faster.) Serve immediately or at room temperature with lemon wedges.

SERVES 4

FRITTELLE DI BACCALÀ

Salt Cod Fritters

Cod from Northern Europe was traditionally preserved in salt for consumption inland. Its popularity in Mediterranean countries is a legacy of meatless 'humility' days observed by the Catholic church.

225 g (8 oz) salt cod
1 small onion, sliced
2 garlic cloves, sliced
1 bay leaf
375 ml (13 fl oz/1½ cups) milk
80 ml (3 fl oz/⅓ cup) dry white vermouth or white wine
200 g (7 oz) potatoes, chopped

2 tablespoons flat-leaf (Italian) parsley, roughly chopped
pinch of nutmeg
1 egg yolk
1 tablespoon plain (all-purpose) flour, plus a little extra for dusting
500 ml (17 fl oz/2 cups) oil, for frying

Soak the salt cod in cold water for 24 hours, changing the water about four times.

Put the onion, garlic, bay leaf, milk and vermouth in a saucepan, season with pepper and bring to the boil. Add the salt cod, reduce the heat and simmer, covered, for 10–15 minutes until the fish is cooked and flakes away from the skin. Leave in the liquid until cool enough to handle. Meanwhile, boil the potatoes until tender, then drain and cool.

Place the fish on a board and flake the flesh away from the skin and bones. Put the flaked fish in a

bowl and add the potato, parsley, nutmeg, egg yolk, flour and a little pepper. Mix well and taste for seasoning – you should not need to add any more salt. Leave in the refrigerator for 15 minutes and then roll into small balls and flatten slightly.

Heat the oil in a frying pan. Dust the fritters with flour and fry in batches in the hot oil for about 2 minutes on each side. Drain on paper towels and serve warm, perhaps with a tomato sauce.

SERVES 4

Chapter 3
MEAT, POULTRY AND GAME

Whether richly sauced or delicately seasoned with herbs, the Italians treat their meat with respect. Dishes use many cuts and parts of the animal and include roasts, meatballs, salami, sausages and cured meat.

POLPETTE AL POMODORO

Italian Meatballs with Tomato Sauce

Just about every Italian home will have their own family recipe for meatballs, or polpette, as they are known. They can be served with pasta or bread. The dish is best made a day in advance to let the flavours blend together.

185 ml (6 fl oz/³⁄₄ cup) olive oil
1 onion, finely chopped
100 g (4 oz/²⁄₃ cup) pine nuts, roughly chopped
3 garlic cloves, crushed
40 g (1¹⁄₂ oz) flat-leaf (Italian) parsley, roughly chopped
5 g (¹⁄₈ oz) basil or rosemary, roughly chopped
2 teaspoons fennel seeds, ground
55 g (2 oz/²⁄₃ cup) fresh breadcrumbs
250 g (9 oz/1 cup) ricotta cheese
25 g (1 oz/¹⁄₄ cup) grated Parmesan cheese

grated zest of 1 large lemon
1 egg
500 g (1 lb 2 oz) minced (ground) pork or beef

SAUCE
800 g (1 lb 12 oz) tomatoes or
   2 x 400 g (14 oz) tins tomatoes
125 ml (4 fl oz/¹⁄₂ cup) red wine

Heat half the olive oil in a saucepan and cook the onion and pine nuts until the onion is soft and the pine nuts are light golden brown. Add the garlic and cook for a few minutes more, then set aside to cool.

Put the herbs, fennel seeds, breadcrumbs, ricotta, Parmesan, lemon zest and egg in a bowl and add the mince. Add the cooled onion and pine nuts, season with salt and pepper and mix briefly until all the ingredients are combined. Test for correct seasoning by frying one meatball and tasting for flavour. Leave the meatball mixture to rest in the refrigerator for at least 30 minutes or overnight.

To make the meatballs, roll about 50 g (2 oz) of mixture into a ball about the size of a walnut and then flatten slightly to make it easier to cook on both sides. Repeat with the rest of the mixture.

Heat the remaining olive oil in a large saucepan and fry the meatballs until golden brown on both sides. If necessary, cook them in two batches to prevent the pan overcrowding. Make sure there is enough oil to prevent the meatballs sticking to the base of the saucepan. Remove the meatballs from the pan.

To make the sauce, if you are using fresh tomatoes, score a cross in the top of each one, plunge them into boiling water for 20 seconds, then drain and peel the skin away from the cross. Finely chop the flesh. Add the tomatoes and wine to the saucepan, season and simmer for 5 minutes. Gently add the meatballs to the sauce and reduce the heat to a gentle simmer. Cover the saucepan and cook for 10 minutes. Leave for 10 minutes before serving.

SERVES 4

Uccelletti Scappati

Veal Birds

The name means literally 'little birds that got away', either because it is flavoured with sage as birds traditionally were, or because it looks like birds on a skewer. You can also grill (broil) the skewers if you prefer, basting frequently with melted butter.

650 g (1 lb 7 oz) sliced leg of veal
90 g (3 oz) pancetta, thinly sliced
50—60 sage leaves

90 g (3 oz) pancetta, cubed
75 g (3 oz) butter

Soak 12 bamboo skewers in cold water for 1 hour.

Place the veal between two sheets of plastic wrap and pound with a meat mallet until the slices are an even thickness. Cut into 6 x 3 cm (2½ x 1¼ in) rectangles and trim the pancetta slices to the same size.

Working in batches, lie the veal pieces out flat on a board and season with pepper. Place a slice of pancetta on each rectangle of veal and then half a sage leaf on top. Roll each veal slice up, starting from one of the shortest ends.

Thread a cube of pancetta onto a skewer, followed by a sage leaf. Thread the skewer through a veal roll to prevent it from unrolling. Thread four more veal rolls onto the skewer, followed by a sage leaf and, finally, another cube of pancetta. Continue in this way with more skewers until all the ingredients are used.

Heat the butter in a large frying pan. When it foams, add the skewers in batches and cook over high heat for about 12 minutes, or until cooked through, turning several times during cooking. Season lightly and serve with fried polenta.

SERVES 6

Right: Roll up the tiny bundles of veal, pancetta and sage and thread onto the skewers so they can't unroll.

Far right: Wedge the bundles in place at either end of the skewer with a sage leaf and cube of pancetta.

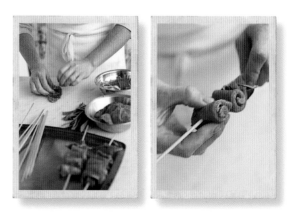

Quaglie in Foglie di Vite

Quails Wrapped in Vine Leaves

4 sprigs of rosemary
4 quails
2 tablespoons olive oil

1 tablespoon balsamic vinegar
2 teaspoons brown sugar
4 large vine leaves

Preheat the oven to 180°C (350°F/Gas 4). Stuff a sprig of rosemary into each quail and then tie its legs together. Tuck the wings behind the back.

Heat the oil in a frying pan and add the quails. Brown them all over and then add the balsamic vinegar and brown sugar and bubble everything together. Remove from the heat.

Blanch the vine leaves in boiling water for about 15 seconds and then wrap one around each quail. Put the wrapped quails in a roasting tin, seam-side down, and bake for 15 minutes.

PICTURE ON OPPOSITE PAGE

SERVES 4

Salsicce e Lenticchie

Sausage and Lentil Stew

3 tablespoons olive oil
850 g (1 lb 14 oz) Italian sausages
1 onion, chopped
3 garlic cloves, thinly sliced
1½ tablespoons chopped rosemary
800 g (1 lb 12 oz) tin chopped tomatoes

16 juniper berries, lightly crushed
pinch of grated nutmeg
1 bay leaf
1 dried chilli, crushed
185 ml (6 fl oz/¾ cup) red wine
95 g (3 oz/½ cup) green lentils

Heat the oil in a large saucepan and cook the sausages for 5–10 minutes, until browned. Remove the sausages from the pan and reduce the heat. Add the onion and garlic to the pan and cook gently until the onion is soft.

Stir in the rosemary, then add the tomatoes and cook gently until reduced to a thick sauce. Add the

juniper berries, nutmeg, bay leaf, chilli, wine and 410 ml (14 fl oz/1⅔ cups) water. Bring to the boil, then add the lentils and sausages. Give the stew a good stir, cover the pan and simmer gently for about 40 minutes, or until the lentils are soft. Stir a couple of times to prevent the lentils sticking to the base of the pan. Add a little more water if the lentils are still not cooked.

SERVES 4

Pollo alla Diavola

Devil's Chicken

Devil's chicken is a dish which originated in the Tuscan kitchen. The chicken is butterflied, then marinated in olive oil and chilli. Traditionally, the bird would be cooked on a grill over an open fire – the flames licking up like the fires of the devil.

2 x 900 g (2 lb) chickens
170 ml (6 fl oz/^{2}/$_3$ cup) olive oil
juice of 1 large lemon
2 sage leaves
3–4 very small red chillies, finely minced,
   or ^{1}/$_2$ teaspoon dried chilli flakes

2 French shallots
2 garlic cloves
4 tablespoons chopped flat-leaf (Italian) parsley
2^1/$_2$ tablespoons softened butter
lemon slices

Split each chicken through the breastbone and press open to form a butterfly, joined down the back. Flatten with your hand to give a uniform surface for cooking. Place in a shallow ovenproof dish large enough to hold both of the chickens side by side.

Mix together the oil, lemon juice, sage and chilli in a bowl and season well with salt and pepper. Pour over the chicken and leave to marinate in the refrigerator for 30 minutes. Turn the chickens and leave for a further 30 minutes.

Meanwhile, chop the shallots, garlic, parsley and butter in a blender or food processor until fine and paste-like. (If you want to do this by hand,

chop the vegetables and then mix them into the softened butter.) Season with salt and pepper. Preheat the grill (broiler).

Place the chickens, skin side down, on a grill (broiler) tray. Position about 10 cm (4 in) below the heat and grill (broil) for 10 minutes, basting with the marinade once or twice. Turn over and grill, basting occasionally, for 10–12 minutes, or until the juices run clear when a thigh is pierced deeply with a skewer.

Spread the butter paste over the skin of the chickens with a knife. Reduce the heat and grill for about 3 minutes until the coating is lightly browned. Serve hot or cold, with lemon wedges.

SERVES 4

Arrange the chickens in a large shallow dish and baste with the marinade while grilling (broiling) them.

Brasato di Maiale al Latte

Pork Braised in Milk

Ask your butcher to chine and skin the pork loin (chining means removing the backbone from the rack of ribs). The milk and lemon sauce will appear lumpy and curdled, but tastes delicious. You can strain it if you like.

1 x 2.25 kg (5 lb) pork loin, chined and skinned
60 ml (2 fl oz/¼ cup) olive oil
4 garlic cloves, cut in half lengthways
15 g (½ oz) sage or rosemary leaves

1 litre (35 fl oz/4 cups) milk
grated zest of 2 lemons
juice of 1 lemon

Preheat the oven to 200°C (400°F/Gas 6). Prepare the pork by trimming the fat to leave just a thin layer. The bone and fat keeps the pork moist.

Heat the olive oil in a large roasting tin. Add the pork loin and brown the meat on all sides. Remove the pork and pour away the fat from the roasting tin. Add the garlic and sage to the tin and place the pork on top. Season with salt and pepper and pour the milk over the pork. Return to the heat and bring just to the boil. Remove the tin from the heat, add the lemon zest and drizzle with the lemon juice.

Transfer the tin to the oven and roast the pork for about 20 minutes. Reduce the temperature to 150°C (300°F/Gas 2) and cook for 1–1¼ hours, depending on the thickness of the meat. Add a little more milk every so often, if necessary, to keep the meat roasting in liquid. Baste the pork with the juices every 30 minutes. Do not cover the meat, so that the juices reduce and the fat on the pork becomes crisp.

To test if the pork is cooked, poke a skewer into the middle of the meat, count to ten and pull it out. Touch it on the inside of your wrist and, if it feels hot, the meat is cooked through. Leave the meat to rest for 10 minutes before carving.

Strain the sauce if you like (you don't need to, but it may look curdled) and serve with the meat. Delicious served with braised fennel, cavolo nero or roasted vegetables.

SERVES 6

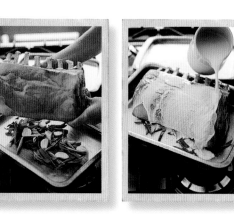

Far left: Putting the garlic and sage in the tin and laying the pork on top makes a rack for the meat to prevent it boiling in its own juices instead of roasting.

Left: Pour the milk over the pork and roast uncovered so the skin crisps.

Osso Buco alla Milanese

Milanese Osso Buco

Osso buco is a Milanese dish and traditionally tomatoes are not used in the cooking of northern Italy. The absence of the robust tomato allows the more delicate flavour of the gremolata to feature in this classic osso buco. Serve with risotto alla Milanese.

12 pieces veal shank, about 4 cm (1½ in) thick
plain (all-purpose) flour, seasoned with salt and pepper
60 ml (2 fl oz/¼ cup) olive oil
60 g (2 oz) butter
1 garlic clove
250 ml (9 fl oz/1 cup) dry white wine
1 bay leaf or lemon leaf
pinch of allspice

pinch of ground cinnamon
thin lemon wedges

GREMOLATA
2 teaspoons grated lemon zest
6 tablespoons finely chopped flat-leaf
  (Italian) parsley
1 garlic clove, finely chopped

Tie each piece of veal around its girth to secure the flesh, then dust with the seasoned flour. Heat the oil, butter and garlic in a large heavy saucepan big enough to hold the shanks in a single layer. Add the shanks and cook for 12–15 minutes until well browned. Arrange the shanks, standing them up in a single layer, pour in the wine and add the bay leaf, allspice and cinnamon. Cover the pan.

Cook at a low simmer for 15 minutes, then add 125 ml (4 fl oz/½ cup) warm water. Continue cooking, covered, for about 45 minutes to 1 hour (the timing will depend on the age of the veal) until the meat is tender and you can cut it with a fork. Check the volume of liquid once or twice and add more warm water as needed. Transfer the veal to a plate and keep warm. Discard the garlic clove and bay leaf from the sauce.

To make the gremolata, mix together the lemon zest, parsley and garlic. Increase the heat under the saucepan and stir for 1–2 minutes until the sauce is thick, scraping up any bits off the bottom of the saucepan as you stir. Stir in the gremolata. Season with salt and pepper if necessary and return the veal to the sauce. Heat through, then serve with the lemon wedges.

SERVES 4

Right: Tie the osso buco to help keep its shape during cooking, then dust it with the seasoned flour.

Far right: The pan for osso buco must be large enough to fit the shank pieces in a single layer so that they cook through evenly.

WINE

The history of wine in Italy stretches back thousands of years. The Etruscans may well have enjoyed wine, though it was the Greeks and later the Romans who saw the real potential in Italy for cultivating vines.

A terrain that ranges from the Alps to the sunbaked south and a Mediterranean climate create a perfect environment for producing a huge variety of unique wines. While today's wines are very different from the rich, aged wines enjoyed by the Romans, there is some continuation in wine-making methods and traditions, particularly in some of Italy's most classic wines – Recioto and Amarone della Valpolicella and Vin Santo, where grapes are dried out before pressing. While the traditional methods are respected and preserved, and many Italian wine producers still consist of a family working their own vineyards, the Italians have also been quick to modernize their cellars and innovative in producing new wines. French grape varieties have been planted alongside the Italian varieties and new technology installed.

Italy's reputation worldwide for its wines was initially based on the easy-drinking bottles of Soave, Frascati, Lambrusco, Asti-Spumante and particularly the distinctive bottles of Chianti, which graced trattorias all over the world. While these wines were very popular and profitable, the quality was variable and in 1963, the Government introduced laws called the denominazione di origine controllata (DOC) to control national wine production. This has led to a rise in standards and to Italy's place as one of the world's leading wine exporters.

Good wines are produced in every one of Italy's regions. Even in the hot South, some excellent wines can be found, while Piemonte and Tuscany produce red wines of international repute. When buying Italian wines, the DOC label guarantees authenticity and certain minimum standards of quality. Some of the country's finest wines, such as Barolo, Barbaresco, Chianti and Brunello di Montalcino are controlled under the much stricter denominazione di origine controllata e garantita (DOCG) regulations, and these wines are often of a very high quality. However, some of Italy's wine makers choose to produce wines that do not conform to the regulations required to obtain DOC status, particularly those regarding grape varieties. There are now attempts to classify these 'super-table' wines, many rating among Italy's finest, under a new IGT (Indicazione Geografica Tipica) system, but many are still sold as just vino da tavola.

In many restaurants in Italy, you may not even be offered a wine list. Instead, the choice is between the house red or white wine. If there is a wine list, you may still choose to pick a local wine, many of which are made to be the perfect partner for the food of their region. Wine is an important part of every meal and is seen as a partner for food, rather than a drink to be drunk on its own.

Roast Turkey with Pistachio Stuffing

Italian roast turkey is traditionally served with mostarda di Cremona, a type of chutney, made from candied fruit such as pear, apricot, melon and orange, preserved with mustard, honey, wine and spices. You can also use this recipe to roast guinea fowl.

STUFFING
45 g (1½ oz) shelled pistachio nuts
100 g (4 oz) prosciutto, finely chopped
225 g (8 oz) minced (ground) pork
225 g (8 oz) minced (ground) chicken
1 egg
80 ml (3 fl oz/⅓ cup) thick (double/heavy) cream
150 g (6 oz) chestnut purée
½ teaspoon finely chopped sage or ¼ teaspoon
   dried sage
pinch of cayenne pepper

1 x 3 kg (6 lb 8 oz) turkey
300 g (11 oz) butter, softened
1 onion, roughly chopped
4 sage leaves
1 sprig of rosemary
½ celery stalk, cut into 2–3 pieces
1 carrot, cut into 3–4 pieces
250 ml (9 fl oz/1 cup) dry white wine
125 ml (4 fl oz/½ cup) dry Marsala
250 ml (9 fl oz/1 cup) chicken stock

To make the stuffing, preheat the oven to 170°C (325°F/Gas 3). Spread the pistachio nuts on a baking tray and toast for 6–8 minutes. Place in a bowl with the other stuffing ingredients, season well and mix together thoroughly.

Fill the turkey cavity with the stuffing and sew up the opening with kitchen string. Cross the legs and tie them together, and tuck the wings behind the body. Rub the skin with 100 g (4 oz) of the butter. Put the onion in the centre of a roasting tin and place the turkey on top, breast up. Add another 100 g (4 oz) of the butter to the tin along with the sage, rosemary, celery and carrot. Pour the white wine and Marsala over the top. Roast for 2½–3 hours, basting several times. Cover the turkey with buttered baking paper when the skin becomes golden brown.

Transfer the turkey to a carving plate and leave to rest in a warm spot. Put the vegetables from the pan into a food processor and blend, or push them through a sieve. Add the pan juices and scrapings from the bottom of the tin and blend until smooth. Transfer the mixture to a saucepan, add the remaining 100 g (4 oz) of butter and the chicken stock and bring to the boil. Season and cook until thickened to a good gravy consistency. Transfer to a gravy boat.

Carve the turkey and serve with stuffing and gravy, and preferably mostarda di Cremona.

SERVES 8

BOLLITO MISTO

Mixed Boiled Meats

This meal requires a trip to a good butcher. If you are lucky enough to find a zampone (pork sausage stuffed into a pig's trotter), use it instead of the cotechino. You will only need a little of the cooking liquid for serving – keep the rest for making soup.

1 x 800 g (1 lb 12 oz) cotechino sausage
1 x 1.25 kg (2 lb 12 oz) small beef tongue
3 sprigs of flat-leaf (Italian) parsley
4 baby carrots
1 celery stalk, sliced
2 onions, roughly chopped
10 peppercorns

2 bay leaves
1 x 1.25 kg (2 lb 12 oz) beef brisket
1 tablespoon tomato paste (concentrated purée)
1 x 900 g (2 lb) chicken
12 whole baby turnips
18 small onions, such as pickling
  or pearl onions

Bring a saucepan of water to the boil. Prick the casing of the cotechino sausage and add to the pan. Reduce the heat, cover the saucepan and simmer for about 1½ hours, or until tender. Leave in the cooking liquid until ready to use.

Meanwhile, bring a stockpot or a very large saucepan of water to the boil. Add the beef tongue, parsley, carrots, celery, chopped onion, peppercorns, bay leaves and 1 teaspoon salt. Return to the boil, skim the surface and add the beef brisket and tomato paste. Cover the pan, then reduce the heat and simmer for 2 hours, skimming the surface from time to time.

Add the chicken, baby turnips and onions to the stockpot and simmer for a further hour. Top up with boiling water if necessary to keep the meat always covered. Add the cotechino for the last 20 minutes of cooking.

Turn off the heat and remove the tongue. Peel, trim and slice it, then arrange the slices on a warm platter. Slice the cotechino and beef and quarter the chicken. Arrange all the meats on the platter and surround them with the carrots, turnips and onions. Moisten with a little of the cooking liquid then take to the table. Serve with green sauce (page 248) and mostarda di Cremona.

SERVES 8

Ragù di Manzo

Beef Ragù

This dish is both starter and main course in one pot. Serve the ragù on spaghetti or bucatini as a first course, and the beef with vegetables or a salad for the main. Ragù is the traditional tomato-based sauce of Bologna.

1 x 1.5 kg (3 lb 5 oz) piece of beef, such as top rump
   or silverside
60 g (2 oz) pork fat, cut into small thin pieces
30 g (1 oz) butter
3 tablespoons olive oil
pinch of cayenne pepper
2 garlic cloves, finely chopped
2 onions, finely chopped
2 carrots, finely chopped
1 celery stalk, finely chopped
1/2 red capsicum (pepper), finely chopped

3 leeks, sliced
185 ml (6 fl oz/3/4 cup) red wine
1 tablespoon tomato paste (concentrated purée)
375 ml (13 fl oz/1 1/2 cups) beef stock
185 ml (6 fl oz/3/4 cup) tomato passata
8 basil leaves, torn into pieces
1/2 teaspoon finely chopped oregano leaves,
   or 1/4 teaspoon dried oregano
2 tablespoons finely chopped flat-leaf (Italian) parsley
60 ml (2 fl oz/1/4 cup) thick (double/heavy) cream

Make deep incisions all over the beef with the point of a sharp knife, then push a piece of pork fat into each incision.

Heat the butter and olive oil in a large casserole and brown the beef for 10–12 minutes, until it is browned all over. Season with salt and then add the cayenne, garlic, onion, carrot, celery, capsicum and leek. Cook over moderate heat for 10 minutes, or until the vegetables are lightly browned.

Increase the heat, add the wine and boil until it has evaporated. Stir in the tomato paste, then add the stock. Simmer for 30 minutes. Add the tomato passata, basil and oregano and season with pepper. Cover the casserole and cook for about 1 hour, or until the beef is tender.

Remove the beef from the casserole and allow it to rest for 10 minutes before carving. Taste the sauce for seasoning and stir in the parsley and cream.

SERVES 6

Far left: The casserole needs to be large enough to hold the beef without it touching the side, so that the sauce can cover the beef completely.

Left: Finish the sauce off with a little cream to make it velvety.

Piccata al Limone

Veal in Lemon and White Wine

4 large veal escalopes
plain (all-purpose) flour, seasoned with salt and pepper
1 tablespoon olive oil
2 tablespoons butter
80 ml (3 fl oz/⅓ cup) dry white wine

250 ml (9 fl oz/1 cup) chicken stock
3 tablespoons lemon juice
2 tablespoons capers, rinsed and chopped if large
1 tablespoon finely chopped flat-leaf (Italian) parsley
8 caperberries

Place the veal between two sheets of plastic wrap and pound with a meat mallet until an even thickness. Lightly dust each side with flour.

Heat the olive oil and butter in a large frying pan. Fry the escalopes over moderately high heat for about 2 minutes on each side, or until golden. Season and transfer to a warm plate.

Add the wine to the pan, increase the heat to high and boil until there are just 3–4 tablespoons of liquid left. Add the stock and boil for 4–5 minutes, or until it has reduced and slightly thickened. Add the lemon juice and capers and cook, stirring, for 1 minute. Taste for seasoning, then return the veal to the frying pan and heat through for 30 seconds. Sprinkle with parsley and serve at once, garnished with caperberries.

PICTURE ON PAGE 104

SERVES 4

Fegato alla Veneziana

Venetian Liver

2 tablespoons olive oil
60 g (2 oz) butter
2 large onions, halved and thinly sliced

600 g (1 lb 5 oz) calves liver, very thinly sliced
1 tablespoon finely chopped flat-leaf (Italian) parsley
lemon wedges

Heat the olive oil and half the butter in a large frying pan and add the onion. Cover and cook over low heat for 30–40 minutes, stirring from time to time, until very soft and golden. Season well with salt and pepper and transfer to a bowl.

Melt the remaining butter in the frying pan, increase the heat and fry the liver quickly until brown on all sides. Return the onion to the pan and cook, stirring often, for 1–2 minutes more, or until the liver is cooked. Remove from the heat, stir in the parsley and check for seasoning. Serve with lemon wedges.

SERVES 4

Veal in Lemon and White Wine (recipe on page 103)

Spezzatino di Agnello

Spicy Lamb Casserole

The pinch of chilli signifies this as a southern dish, probably from Basilicata, where sheep were the main source of income. Such dishes often originated with shepherds, who used wild herbs and vegetables found around their camp.

3 tablespoons olive oil
1.25 kg (2 lb 12 oz) lamb leg or shoulder, cut into
   4 cm (1½ in) cubes
1 small onion, finely chopped
1 celery stalk, finely chopped
3 garlic cloves, crushed
125 ml (4 fl oz/½ cup) dry Marsala
¾ teaspoon chilli flakes

1 tablespoon crushed juniper berries
2 tablespoons tomato paste (concentrated purée)
250 ml (9 fl oz/1 cup) chicken stock
1 sprig of rosemary
12 small onions, such as cipolline or pearl onions
2 potatoes, cut into cubes
2 tablespoons finely chopped flat-leaf (Italian) parsley

Preheat the oven to 180°C (350°F/Gas 4). Heat the olive oil in a large casserole. Add the lamb cubes in batches, so that you don't overcrowd the pan, season with salt and pepper and brown lightly over high heat. Remove each batch from the casserole as it browns. Once all the lamb is browned and has been removed from the casserole, add the chopped onion, celery and garlic, reduce the heat and cook for 4–5 minutes until softened.

Return the lamb to the casserole. Pour in the Marsala and cook over high heat until it is dark brown and reduced by half. Add the chilli flakes and juniper berries and cook, stirring, for just 10–15 seconds. Add the tomato paste, chicken stock, rosemary and about 250 ml (9 fl oz/1 cup) water, or enough to just cover.

Cover the casserole with a lid and bake in the oven for 45 minutes. Add the onions and potato and cook for another 45 minutes. Stir the parsley through just before serving.

SERVES 4

ARROSTO DI AGNELLO

Roast Lamb

This recipe can also be used for roasting a leg of veal or a rib or loin of lamb or veal. For lamb, follow the cooking times in the recipe. You will need to roast the veal for 25 minutes per 450 grams (1 pound), plus an extra 10 minutes.

2 sprigs of rosemary
3 garlic cloves
75 g (3 oz) pancetta
1 x 2 kg (4 lb 8 oz) leg of lamb, shank bone cut off just
  above the joint and trimmed of excess fat

1 large onion, cut into 4 thick slices
125 ml (4 fl oz/½ cup) olive oil
375 ml (13 fl oz/1½ cups) dry white wine

Preheat the oven to 230°C (450°F/Gas 8).

Strip the leaves off the rosemary sprigs and chop with the garlic and pancetta until fine and paste-like (a food processor works well for this). Season with a little salt and plenty of pepper.

With the point of a sharp knife, make incisions about 1 cm (½ in) deep all over the lamb. Rub the rosemary filling over the surface of the lamb, pressing it into the incisions.

Put the onion slices in the centre of a roasting tin. Place the lamb on top and gently pour the olive oil over it. Roast the lamb for 15 minutes. Reduce the temperature to 180°C (350°F/Gas 4) and pour in 250 ml (9 fl oz/1 cup) of the white wine. Roast for 1 hour for medium-rare, or longer if you prefer. Baste the meat a couple of times and add a little water if the juices start to burn. Transfer the lamb to a carving platter and leave to rest for 10 minutes.

Discard the onion slices and spoon off the excess fat from the roasting tin. Place over high heat on the stovetop, pour in the remaining wine and cook for 3–4 minutes, or until the sauce reduces and slightly thickens. Taste for seasoning.

Slice the lamb and serve on a warm serving platter with the sauce spooned over the top.

SERVES 4

Right: Use a sharp knife to push the rosemary filling into the incisions on the surface of the lamb.

Far right: Baste a couple of times while the meat is roasting.

Pollo alla Cacciatora

Chicken Cacciatore

Just like the French chasseur, cacciatora means 'hunter's style'. The dish is originally from central Italy, but like so much Italian fare, every region has put its own twist on the recipe. This one, with tomatoes, is probably the most widely travelled.

3 tablespoons olive oil
1 large onion, finely chopped
3 garlic cloves, crushed
1 celery stalk, finely chopped
150 g (6 oz) pancetta, finely chopped
125 g (5 oz) button mushrooms, thickly sliced
4 chicken drumsticks

4 chicken thighs
80 ml (3 fl oz/⅓ cup) dry vermouth or dry white wine
2 x 400 g (14 oz) tins chopped tomatoes
¼ teaspoon brown sugar
1 sprig of oregano, plus 4–5 sprigs to garnish
1 sprig of rosemary
1 bay leaf

Heat half the olive oil in a large casserole. Add the onion, garlic and celery and cook, stirring from time to time, over moderately low heat for 6–8 minutes until the onion is golden.

Add the pancetta and mushrooms to the casserole, increase the heat and cook, stirring occasionally, for 4–5 minutes. Spoon onto a plate and set aside.

Add the remaining olive oil to the casserole and lightly brown the chicken pieces, a few at a time. Season them as they brown. Spoon off any excess fat and return all the pieces to the casserole. Add the vermouth, increase the heat and cook until the liquid has almost evaporated.

Add the tomatoes, sugar, oregano, rosemary, bay leaf and 80 ml (3 fl oz/⅓ cup) cold water. Bring to the boil then stir in the reserved pancetta mixture. Cover and leave to simmer for 20 minutes, or until the chicken is tender but not falling off the bone.

If the liquid is too thin, remove the chicken pieces from the casserole, increase the heat and boil until thickened. Discard the sprigs of herbs and taste for salt and pepper. Toss in the extra oregano sprigs and the dish is ready to serve.

SERVES 4

Spezzatino di Cervo

Venison Casserole

A dark gamey meat like venison needs strong flavours to balance it. This casserole contains cloves, juniper and allspice – all robust flavourings in their own right. Serve with creamy polenta or potatoes to mop up the rich gravy.

1 sprig of rosemary
1 large onion
1 garlic clove
85 g (3 oz) prosciutto
100 g (4 oz) butter
1 kg (2 lb 4 oz) venison, cut into large cubes
1 litre (35 fl oz/4 cups) beef stock
80 ml (3 fl oz/⅓ cup) red wine vinegar
80 ml (3 fl oz/⅓ cup) robust red wine

2 cloves
4 juniper berries
pinch of allspice
1 bay leaf
3 tablespoons plain (all-purpose) flour
2 tablespoons dry Marsala or brandy
1½ teaspoons grated lemon zest
1½ tablespoons finely chopped flat-leaf (Italian) parsley

Strip the leaves off the rosemary and chop them finely with the onion, garlic and prosciutto. Heat half the butter in a large heavy saucepan with a lid. Add the rosemary mixture and soften over moderately low heat for 5 minutes. Season with pepper. Increase the heat, add the venison and cook for 10 minutes, or until brown on all sides.

Put the stock in another saucepan and bring to the boil, then reduce the heat and keep at a low simmer.

Increase the heat under the venison, add the vinegar and cook until the liquid becomes thick and syrupy. Pour in the red wine. When that becomes syrupy, stir in half of the simmering stock. Add the cloves, juniper berries, allspice and bay leaf and cover the

pan. Simmer for 1 hour, stirring once or twice and adding a little hot water if necessary to maintain the liquid level.

Meanwhile, melt the remaining 50 g (2 oz) of butter in a saucepan. Stir in the flour and cook over moderately low heat for 1 minute. Slowly stir in the remaining stock and cook until the sauce thickens slightly.

Stir the sauce into the casserole, then add the Marsala. Uncover the pan and simmer for a further 20 minutes. Taste for salt and pepper. Mix together the lemon zest and parsley and sprinkle over the top before serving.

SERVES 4

Involtini di Vitello

Veal Rolls

Involtini means 'little bundles' and if you travel around Italy you'll find this recipe in many guises. Traditionally involtini were made with meat or fish, stuffed with breadcrumbs, pine nuts and currants. You could also use turkey or chicken breast.

8 asparagus spears
4 veal escalopes
4 thin slices mortadella (preferably with pistachio nuts)
4 thin slices Bel Paese

plain (all-purpose) flour, seasoned with salt and pepper
3 tablespoons butter
1 tablespoon olive oil
3 tablespoons dry Marsala

Wash the asparagus and remove the woody ends (hold each spear at both ends and bend gently – it will snap at its natural breaking point). Blanch the asparagus in boiling salted water for 3 minutes. Drain, reserving 3 tablespoons of the liquid.

Place each veal escalope between two sheets of plastic wrap and pound with a meat mallet to a 12 x 18 cm (5 x 7 in) rectangle. Season lightly with salt and pepper. Trim the mortadella and cheese slices to just a little smaller than the veal.

Cover each piece of veal with a slice of mortadella, then a slice of cheese. Place an asparagus spear in the centre, running across the shortest width, with the tip slightly overhanging the veal at one end. Place another asparagus spear alongside, but with its tip overhanging the other end. Roll each veal slice up tightly and tie in place at each end with kitchen string. Roll in the seasoned flour to coat.

Heat 2 tablespoons of the butter with the olive oil in a frying pan. Fry the rolls over low heat for about 10 minutes, turning frequently, until golden and tender. Transfer to a hot serving dish and keep warm.

Add the Marsala, the reserved asparagus liquid and the remaining butter to the pan and bring quickly to the boil. Simmer for 3–4 minutes, scraping up the bits from the base of the pan. The juices will reduce and darken. Taste for seasoning, then spoon over the veal rolls and serve immediately.

SERVES 4

Far left: Escalopes of veal are usually pounded with a meat mallet before use, giving a thin tender meat that can be wrapped around fillings and fried quickly.

Left: Tie the involtini with kitchen string to prevent them from unravelling while they're frying.

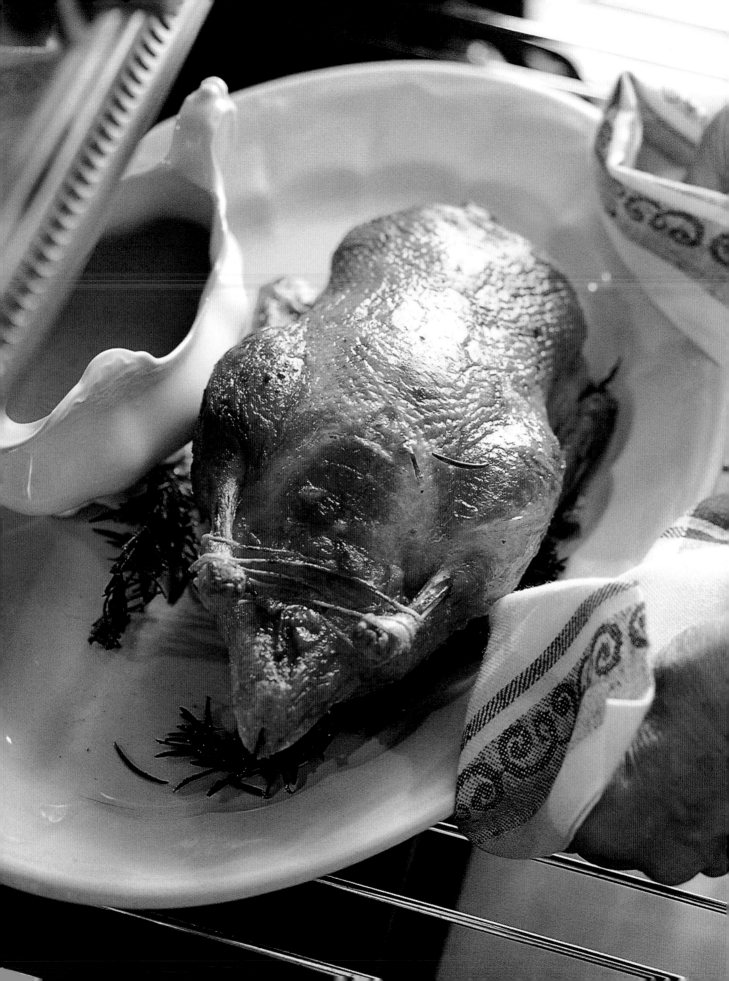

Anatra al Forno con Prosciutto

Roast Duck with Parma Ham

Parma ham was supposedly served to Hannibal at a banquet in the city in 217 BC. Today its production is a licensed industry, with only ham from the Emilia-Romagna region taking the name, and the ducal crown of Parma branded on the skin.

2 thick slices 'country-style' bread, such as ciabatta, crusts removed
125 ml (4 fl oz/½ cup) milk
1 x 2 kg (4 lb 8 oz) duck
6 thick slices Parma ham
3 garlic cloves, crushed
125 g (5 oz) minced (ground) pork
125 g (5 oz) minced (ground) veal
2 French shallots, finely chopped

2 tablespoons grated Parmesan cheese
1 tablespoon finely chopped flat-leaf (Italian) parsley
1 egg
80 ml (3 fl oz/⅓ cup) olive oil
60 g (2 oz) lard or butter
2 sprigs of rosemary
4 tablespoons grappa or brandy
250 ml (9 fl oz/1 cup) chicken stock
3 tablespoons thick (double/heavy) cream

Preheat the oven to 220°C (425°F/Gas 7). Soak the bread in the milk. Remove any excess skin and fat from the duck, leaving just enough skin to sew the cavity closed later.

Bring a large saucepan of water to the boil. Prick the skin of the duck all over and put it into the boiling water with a teaspoon of salt. Boil for 12 minutes. Remove the duck and place, cavity-side down, in a colander to drain for 10 minutes. Dry the duck well all over, inside and out, with paper towels.

Finely chop 2 slices of the Parma ham and mix it with the garlic, minced pork and veal, shallots, Parmesan and parsley. Squeeze the bread dry and add to the mixture. Add the egg, season and mix well. Fill the duck cavity with the stuffing then stitch closed with kitchen string. Tie the wings and legs together with string.

Put the oil, lard and rosemary in a roasting tin and heat in the oven for 5 minutes. Put the duck in the middle, breast up, and roast for 10 minutes. Baste with the pan juices and lay the remaining slices of Parma ham over the breast, covering the legs as well. Reduce the heat to 190°C (375°F/Gas 5) and roast for a further hour, basting several times. Remove the Parma ham, increase the heat to 210°C (415°F/Gas 6–7) and return to the oven for 10 minutes.

Transfer the duck to a carving plate to rest for 10 minutes. Spoon the fat out of the roasting tin, leaving just the duck juices, and place the tin over high heat on the stove. Add the grappa and cook until it is syrupy and almost evaporated, then add the stock. Continue boiling until slightly thickened, then add the cream. Season well and strain into a sauceboat. Remove the string, carve the duck and stir any juices into the sauce before serving.

SERVES 4

Chapter 4

VEGETABLES

⦿⦿⦿

The mainstay of Italian cooking, vegetables mark the passing of the seasons. Served as meals in their own right, they are chargrilled, fried, marinated or used for sauces. Contorni are vegetables served as side dishes.

Torta di Verdure
Vegetable Torte

150 g (6 oz) asparagus
4 tablespoons olive oil
1 onion, chopped
1 zucchini (courgette), halved lengthways and
  thinly sliced
2 large garlic cloves, crushed

100 g (4 oz) spinach, stalks removed if necessary
1 tablespoon chopped basil
75 g (3 oz/$\frac{3}{4}$ cup) grated Parmesan cheese
250 g (9 oz/1 cup) ricotta cheese
250 g (9 oz) mascarpone cheese
4 eggs

Wash the asparagus and remove the woody ends (hold each spear at both ends and bend gently – it will snap at its natural breaking point). Remove the spear tips of the asparagus and slice the stems. Bring a small saucepan of salted water to the boil and cook the asparagus stems for about 2 minutes. Add the tips and cook for 1 minute. Drain the asparagus and set aside.

Preheat the oven to 180°C (375°F/Gas 4). Heat the oil in a saucepan and cook the onion until soft. Increase the heat and add the zucchini. Cook until the zucchini is softened and golden brown, stirring occasionally. Add the garlic and cook for 1 minute more. Finally, add the spinach and mix briefly until just wilted.

Remove the pan from the heat, add the asparagus and the basil, season with salt and pepper and set aside to cool.

Grease a 20 cm (8 in) springform tin with butter and dust with about 1 tablespoon of the Parmesan. Mix together the ricotta, mascarpone, eggs and 50 g (2 oz/$\frac{1}{2}$ cup) of the Parmesan and add it to the cooled vegetable mixture. Mix well and taste for seasoning.

Spoon the mixture into the tin and scatter with the remaining Parmesan. Place in the oven, on a tray to catch any drips, and cook for 30 minutes. The top should be light golden brown and the mixture should still wobble slightly in the centre. Leave to cool for 30 minutes, then chill in the refrigerator for 3 hours, until the torte has set. Serve with a simple rocket (arugula) or mixed leaf salad.

SERVES 4

Radicchio alla Brace
Chargrilled Radicchio

2 heads radicchio
60 ml (2 fl oz/¼ cup) olive oil

1 teaspoon balsamic vinegar

Trim the radicchio, discarding the outer leaves. Slice into quarters lengthways and rinse well. Drain, then pat dry with paper towels.

Preheat a chargrill pan (griddle) to hot. Lightly sprinkle the radicchio with some of the olive oil and season with salt and pepper.

Cook the radicchio for 2–3 minutes, or until the under leaves soften and darken, then turn to cook the other side. Transfer to a serving dish and then sprinkle with the remaining oil and the vinegar. Serve with grilled (broiled) meats, or cold as part of an antipasto platter.

PICTURE ON OPPOSITE PAGE

SERVES 4

Borlotti Brasati
Braised Borlotti Beans

These beans are best eaten warm or cold rather than piping hot straight from the stove. They keep well in the refrigerator for up to six days, but, if you are making them in advance, don't add the parsley until you are ready to serve.

350 g (12 oz) dried borlotti beans
440 ml (15 fl oz/1¾ cups) dry red wine
1 small onion, finely chopped
3 cloves
125 ml (4 fl oz/½ cup) olive oil

1 sprig of rosemary
3 garlic cloves, crushed
pinch of chilli flakes
3 tablespoons chopped flat-leaf (Italian) parsley

Soak the borlotti beans in cold water overnight, then drain. Place in a large saucepan and add the wine, onion, cloves, half the olive oil and 875 ml (31 fl oz/3½ cups) water. Cover and bring to the boil, then reduce the heat and simmer, uncovered, for 1 hour.

Heat the remaining oil in a small saucepan. Strip the leaves off the rosemary sprig and chop them

finely. Place in the oil with the garlic and chilli and cook for 1 minute. Add to the beans and simmer for 30 minutes to 1 hour, until the beans are tender.

Drain the beans, reserving the cooking liquid. Return the cooking liquid to the pan and simmer until it thickens. Season. Return the beans to the pan and simmer for a further 5 minutes. Stir in the parsley and cool for 15 minutes before serving.

SERVES 6

ZUCCHE E PATATE GRATINATE
Pumpkin and Potato Gratin

450 g (1 lb) potatoes, thinly sliced
leaves from 3 large sprigs of thyme or rosemary,
  finely chopped

700 g (1 lb 9 oz) pumpkin (squash), thinly sliced
1 large garlic clove, crushed
500 ml (17 fl oz/2 cups) thick (double/heavy) cream

Preheat the oven to 180°C (375°F/Gas 4). Lightly grease a 25 x 23 cm (10 x 9 in) gratin dish with a little butter. Arrange a layer of potato in the dish, season with salt, pepper and herbs, then top with a layer of pumpkin. Continue the layers, finishing with pumpkin. Mix the garlic with the cream and pour over the top. Cover the dish with buttered foil and bake for about 45 minutes.

Test to see if the gratin is cooked by inserting a knife into the centre. If the slices seem soft, it is cooked. Remove the foil and increase the oven temperature to 190°C (375°F/Gas 5). Cook for a further 15 minutes, until there is a good brown crust on top. Leave to rest for at least 10 minutes before serving. Delicious with grilled (broiled) meats or on its own with just a green salad.

SERVES 4

TORTA DI PATATE
Potato Torte

The South of Italy loves its pasta, while the North favours rice and polenta. Potato will never be the staple it is in other countries, but there are still some traditional recipes.

1 small onion, thinly sliced into rings
75 g (3 oz) butter
2 garlic cloves, crushed
1 kg (2 lb 4 oz) potatoes, thinly sliced

100 g (4 oz/²/₃ cup) grated mozzarella cheese
50 g (2 oz/¹/₂ cup) grated Parmesan cheese
2 tablespoons milk

Place the onion in a bowl, cover with cold water and leave for 1 hour. Drain well. Preheat the oven to 210°C (415°F/Gas 6–7). Line a 20 cm (8 in) springform cake tin with foil. Grease the foil.

Melt the butter in a small saucepan, add the garlic and set aside. Place a layer of potato in the tin, followed by layers of onion, butter, mozzarella and Parmesan. Repeat the layers until you have used all

the ingredients, finishing with potato and keeping a bit of butter to drizzle on at the end. Season the layers as you go. Spoon the milk over the top.

Bake for 1 hour, or until the top is golden brown and the potato is tender. If the top is overbrowning before the potatoes are done, cover with foil. Cool for 10 minutes, then remove the base of the tin and the foil. Transfer to a warm plate to serve.

SERVES 4

La Bandiera

Tri-coloured Pasta

La Bandiera is the name of the Italian flag. This dish, from Puglia in Italy's south, contains tomatoes, rocket and pasta – the red, green and white ingredients mimic the colours of the flag.

2 potatoes, cut into cubes
300 g (11 oz) ditali, pennette or maccheroncini rigati
4 tablespoons olive oil
3 garlic cloves, crushed
½ teaspoon minced anchovy fillets
2 x 400 g (14 oz) tins tomatoes, roughly chopped

¼ teaspoon sugar
2 tablespoons chopped basil leaves
40 g (1½ oz) rocket (arugula) leaves, torn into small
   pieces if large
2 tablespoons grated pecorino cheese, plus extra
   for serving

Put a large saucepan of water on to boil. Add the potato with 1 teaspoon salt. When the potato has been boiling for 3–4 minutes, stir the pasta into the water and cook until al dente.

Meanwhile, heat the oil, garlic and anchovies in a large frying pan over low heat for 30 seconds. Before the garlic colours, add the tomato, sugar

and basil. Increase the heat, season with salt and pepper and simmer until the pasta in the other pan has finished cooking.

Drain the potato and pasta and add to the tomato sauce. Add the rocket and pecorino cheese, toss to coat and serve at once, with a little extra grated pecorino over the top.

PICTURE ON PAGE 130

SERVES 4

Patate al Forno con Rosmarino

Roasted Rosemary Potatoes

80 ml (3 fl oz/⅓ cup) extra virgin olive oil
750 g (1 lb 10 oz) floury potatoes, cut into 4 cm
   (1½ in) cubes

long sprig of rosemary
sea salt

Preheat the oven to 170°C (325°F/Gas 3). Pour the olive oil into a shallow casserole or baking tray. Toss the potato into the casserole, turning to coat thoroughly in oil, then spread out so that the pieces aren't touching. Scatter the rosemary leaves over the potatoes.

Roast the potatoes for 30 minutes, then turn and sprinkle generously with sea salt. Return to the oven and roast for a further 30–40 minutes, or until crisp and golden. Serve hot or cold.

SERVES 4

Tri-coloured Pasta (recipe on page 129)

Melanzane alla Parmigiana

Eggplant Parmigiana

Parmigiana is a deceptive name for this dish, as the recipe does not, in fact, hail from that city. Instead its creation is claimed by almost every region of Italy, but the use of mozzarella and tomatoes indicates a dish from the south.

1.5 kg (3 lb 5 oz) eggplants (aubergines)
plain (all-purpose) flour
330 ml (12 fl oz/1⅓ cups) olive oil
500 ml (17 fl oz/2 cups) tomato passata

2 tablespoons roughly torn basil leaves
250 g (9 oz/1⅔ cups) grated mozzarella cheese
100 g (4 oz/1 cup) grated Parmesan cheese

Thinly slice the eggplants lengthways. Layer the slices in a large colander, sprinkling salt between each layer. Leave for 1 hour to extract the bitter juices. Rinse and pat the slices dry on both sides with paper towels. Coat the eggplant slices lightly with flour.

Preheat the oven to 180°C (350°F/Gas 4). Grease a 32 x 20 cm (13 x 8 in) shallow casserole or a baking tray.

Heat 125 ml (4 fl oz/½ cup) of the oil in a large frying pan. Quickly fry the eggplant in batches over moderately high heat until crisp and golden on both sides. Add more olive oil as needed, and drain well on paper towels as you remove each batch from the pan.

Make a slightly overlapping layer of eggplant slices over the base of the casserole. Season with pepper. Spoon 4 tablespoons of passata over the eggplant and scatter a few pieces of basil on top. Sprinkle with some mozzarella, followed by some Parmesan. Continue with this layering until you have used up all the ingredients.

Bake for 30 minutes. Remove from the oven and allow to cool for 30 minutes before serving.

SERVES 8

Far left: Frying the eggplant (aubergine) slices first adds flavour to the finished dish.

Left: Layer the eggplant slices, passata, basil, mozzarella and Parmesan in the casserole.

PATATE E PORRI GRATINATI
Potato and Leek Gratin

3 tablespoons butter
400 g (14 oz) leeks, trimmed, halved and sliced
3 garlic cloves, thinly sliced
1 tablespoon chopped thyme

1 kg (2 lb 4 oz) potatoes, thinly sliced
350 g (12 oz) mascarpone cheese
250 ml (9 fl oz/1 cup) vegetable stock

Preheat the oven to 180°C (375°F/Gas 4). Heat the butter in a saucepan and cook the leeks for 10 minutes, or until soft. Season, add the garlic and thyme and cook for a couple of minutes.

Grease a 20 cm (8 in) round gratin dish with butter. Arrange a layer of potato in the base of the dish and season with salt and pepper. Scatter with

3 tablespoons of leek and a few dollops of the mascarpone. Continue the layers, finishing with a layer of potato and some mascarpone. Pour the stock over the top and cover with foil.

Bake for 45 minutes, then remove the foil. Bake for a further 15 minutes to brown the top.

PICTURE ON OPPOSITE PAGE

SERVES 4

FAGIOLI ALL'UCCELLETTO
White Beans with Tomato and Sage

350 g (12 oz) dried cannellini beans
bouquet garni
125 ml (4 fl oz/½ cup) olive oil
2 garlic cloves

1 sprig of sage, or ½ teaspoon dried sage
4 ripe tomatoes, peeled and chopped
1 tablespoon balsamic vinegar

Soak the cannellini beans in cold water overnight, then drain. Place in a large saucepan of cold water with the bouquet garni and bring to the boil. Add 2 tablespoons of the olive oil, then reduce the heat and simmer for 1 hour. Add 1 teaspoon of salt and 500 ml (17 fl oz/2 cups) boiling water and cook for a further 30 minutes, or until tender. Drain.

Cut the garlic cloves in half and put in a large saucepan with the sage and the remaining oil.

Gently heat to infuse the flavours, but do not fry. Add the tomato and simmer for 10 minutes, then discard the garlic and the sprig of sage.

Add the cannellini beans, season well and simmer for 15 minutes. Add a little boiling water at first to help keep the pan moist, but then let the liquid evaporate towards the end of cooking. Stir the vinegar through just before serving. Serve hot.

SERVES 6

Chapter 5

PIZZA AND FOCACCIA

⌀⌀⌀⌀⌀⌀⌀⌀⌀⌀⌀⌀⌀⌀⌀⌀⌀⌀⌀⌀⌀⌀⌀⌀⌀⌀⌀⌀⌀⌀⌀⌀

The Italian pizza has become a universal favourite, the thin, crisp base a foundation for myriad toppings. Country-style breads such as focaccia can, with a few olives and cooked meats, become a meal in their own right.

Pizza Quattro Stagioni

Four Seasons Pizza

1 x 30 cm (12 in) pizza base (page 245)
cornmeal
1 quantity tomato sauce (page 244)
1 tablespoon grated Parmesan cheese
60 g (2 oz) mozzarella cheese, chopped
30 g (1 oz) thinly sliced prosciutto, cut into small pieces
1 Roma (plum) tomato, thinly sliced

3 basil leaves, shredded
4 small artichoke hearts, marinated in oil, drained and quartered
4 button mushrooms, sliced
pinch of dried oregano
1 tablespoon olive oil

Preheat the oven to 240°C (475°F/Gas 9). Put the pizza base on a baking tray dusted with cornmeal. Spoon the tomato sauce onto the base, spreading it up to the rim. Sprinkle the Parmesan on top.

Visually divide the pizza into quarters and scatter the mozzarella over two of the opposite quarters. Spread the prosciutto pieces over one of these, and arrange the tomato slices over the other. Lightly salt the tomato and sprinkle on the basil. Arrange the artichoke quarters over the third quarter, and then mushrooms over the final quarter. Sprinkle the oregano over both these sections.

Drizzle the olive oil over the pizza and bake for 12–15 minutes, or until golden and puffed.

PICTURE ON OPPOSITE PAGE

MAKES ONE PIZZA

Pizza Spinaci

Spinach Pizza

2 tablespoons olive oil
2 garlic cloves, crushed
2 tablespoons pine nuts
1 kg (2 lb 4 oz) spinach, roughly chopped
1 x 30 cm (12 in) pizza base (page 245)

cornmeal
1 quantity tomato sauce (page 244)
220 g (8 oz) mozzarella cheese, chopped
15 very small black olives, such as Ligurian
3 tablespoons grated Parmesan cheese

Preheat the oven to 240°C (475°F/Gas 9). Heat the oil in a frying pan and fry the garlic and pine nuts over low heat until golden. Add the spinach, increase the heat and stir until wilted. Season.

Place the pizza base on a baking tray dusted with cornmeal. Spoon the tomato sauce onto the base, spreading it up to the rim. Sprinkle with half the mozzarella. Spread the spinach and olives over the top, then the rest of the mozzarella and Parmesan.

Bake the pizza for 12–15 minutes, or until golden and puffed. Brush the rim with a little extra olive oil before serving.

MAKES ONE PIZZA

CALZONE

Folded Pizza

Calzone differs from a pizza in that the base is folded over the topping. This Neapolitan speciality means 'trouser leg', presumably because there is a resemblance. Each of the following fillings makes one 25 cm (10 in) calzone – enough for one to two people.

cornmeal
½ quantity pizza dough (page 245) for each calzone
1½ tablespoons olive oil

MOZZARELLA AND PROSCIUTTO
170 g (6 oz) mozzarella cheese, cut into
   2 cm (¾ in) cubes
2 thin slices prosciutto, cut in half
1 artichoke heart, marinated in oil, drained and
   cut into 3 slices from top to bottom

POTATO, ONION AND SALAMI
2 tablespoons vegetable oil
1 small onion, very thinly sliced
75 g (3 oz) small red potatoes, unpeeled,
   very thinly sliced
75 g (3 oz) mozzarella cheese, chopped
60 g (2 oz) sliced salami
2 tablespoons grated Parmesan cheese

Preheat the oven to 230°C (450°F/Gas 8). Lightly oil a baking tray and dust with cornmeal.

On a lightly floured surface, roll out the dough into an 18 cm (7 in) circle. Next, using the heels of your hands and working from the centre outwards, press the circle out to a diameter of 30 cm (12 in). Transfer to the baking tray and brush the entire surface lightly with the oil.

To make the mozzarella and prosciutto calzone, spread the mozzarella cheese over one half of the pizza base, leaving a narrow border around the edge. Roll the half slices of prosciutto into little tubes and place on top of the cheese. Top with the artichoke slices, then season well.

To make the potato, onion and salami calzone, heat the oil in a frying pan and add the onion slices. Cook for 1 minute, then scatter the potato on top. Cook, stirring, for 3–4 minutes, or until beginning to brown. Season with salt and pepper. Spread over one half of the pizza base, leaving a narrow border around the edge. Scatter the mozzarella on top, followed by the salami slices and Parmesan.

Whichever calzone you are making, now fold the plain side of the base over the filling to make a half-moon shape. Match the cut edges and press them firmly together to seal. Fold them over and press into a scrolled pattern to thoroughly seal in the filling. Brush the surface with a little extra olive oil, then transfer to the oven. Bake for about 20 minutes, or until the crust is golden.

EACH RECIPE MAKES ONE 25 CM (10 IN) CALZONE

Focaccia con Pancetta e Parmigiana
Focaccia with Pancetta and Parmesan

One quantity of the focaccia dough (page 246) makes two focaccia. Each of these recipes is for one focaccia, so you can make both types with one quantity of dough.

½ quantity focaccia dough (page 246), rolled out
  and on a tray
90 g (3 oz) pancetta, diced

10 basil leaves, torn in half
olive oil
2 tablespoons grated Parmesan cheese

Preheat the oven to 220°C (425°F/Gas 7). When the dough has risen the second time, scatter the pancetta over the surface and press the pieces firmly into the focaccia dough. Press a piece of basil into each indentation. Brush the surface of the dough with olive oil, sprinkle with Parmesan and bake for about 20 minutes, or until golden.

PICTURE ON OPPOSITE PAGE

MAKES ONE FOCACCIA

Focaccia con Olive Verdi e Rosmarino
Focaccia with Green Olives and Rosemary

½ quantity focaccia dough (page 246), rolled out
  and on a tray
175 g (6 oz/1 cup) green olives

olive oil
2 teaspoons coarse sea salt
leaves of 2 sprigs of rosemary

Preheat the oven to 220°C (425°F/Gas 7). When the dough has risen the second time, scatter the olives over the surface and press them firmly into the focaccia dough. Brush with olive oil and sprinkle with the sea salt and rosemary leaves. Bake for about 20 minutes, or until golden.

MAKES ONE FOCACCIA

Pizza Margherita

Tomato and Cheese Pizza

This classic pizza was supposedly invented in 1889 by Raffaele Esposito in honour of Queen Margherita. The Queen had heard so much of the fabled pizzas of Naples that she requested one to eat when she visited the city.

1 x 30 cm (12 in) pizza base (page 245)
cornmeal
1 quantity tomato sauce (page 244)

150 g (6 oz) mozzarella cheese, chopped
9 small basil leaves
1 tablespoon olive oil

Preheat the oven to 240°C (475°F/Gas 9). Place the pizza base on a baking tray dusted with cornmeal and spoon the tomato sauce onto the base, spreading it up to the rim. Scatter with the mozzarella and basil and drizzle with the oil.

Bake for 12–15 minutes, or until golden and puffed. Remove from the oven and brush the rim with a little extra olive oil before serving.

PICTURE ON OPPOSITE PAGE

MAKES ONE PIZZA

Pizza Melanzana

Eggplant Pizza

220 g (8 oz) long thin eggplants (aubergines), thinly sliced
80 ml (3 fl oz/⅓ cup) olive oil
1 x 30 cm (12 in) pizza base (page 245)
cornmeal
1 quantity tomato sauce (page 244), made with a pinch of chilli flakes

170 g (6 oz) mozzarella cheese, chopped
15 black olives
1 tablespoon capers
4 tablespoons grated pecorino cheese

Layer the eggplant in a colander, sprinkling salt between each layer. Leave to drain for 1 hour. Wipe off the salt with paper towels. Preheat the oven to 240°C (475°F/Gas 8).

Heat 3 tablespoons of the oil in a large frying pan. Quickly brown the eggplant on both sides, cooking in batches. Drain on paper towels.

Put the pizza base on a baking tray dusted with cornmeal. Spoon the tomato sauce onto the base, spreading it up to the rim. Arrange the eggplant in a circular pattern over the top, then scatter with the chopped mozzarella. Sprinkle with the olives, capers and grated pecorino, then drizzle with the remaining oil. Bake the pizza for 12–15 minutes, or until golden and puffed.

MAKES ONE PIZZA

PIZZETTE

Small Pizzas

½ quantity pizza dough (page 245)
cornmeal
250 g (9 oz) mozzarella cheese
1 tablespoon olive oil

GARLIC AND ROSEMARY PIZZETTE

4 garlic cloves, crushed
2 teaspoons chopped rosemary
1½ tablespoons olive oil
50 g (2 oz) grated Parmesan cheese
3 garlic cloves, thinly sliced

TOMATO AND OLIVE PIZZETTE

200 g (7 oz) pitted black olives, diced
400 g (14 oz) Roma (plum) tomatoes, diced
3 garlic cloves, crushed
2 tablespoons finely shredded basil
3 tablespoons olive oil
5 small sprigs of basil

Preheat the oven to 240°C (475°F/Gas 9). Form the pizza dough into ten bases. Place the pizza bases on two baking trays dusted with cornmeal. Grate the mozzarella cheese. Brush the pizza bases with the oil, then sprinkle with mozzarella. Make five garlic and rosemary pizzette and five tomato and olive pizzette.

To make the garlic and rosemary pizzette, scatter five bases with the crushed garlic and rosemary and drizzle with the oil. Sprinkle with Parmesan and garnish with some slices of garlic.

To make the tomato and olive pizzette, mix together the olives, tomato, garlic and shredded basil and spoon over the remaining bases. Drizzle with the oil and garnish with the basil sprigs.

Bake the pizzette for 10 minutes, or until the bases are crisp and golden.

MAKES 10 PIZZETTE

Pizza

Pizza began life as a fast food, eaten hot on the backstreets of Naples. Today it is found all over the world, but it is still in Naples that skilled pizzaioli (pizza-makers) use wonderful local tomatoes, mozzarella and basil to produce the finest of pizzas.

Pizza, in the sense of a flat bread covered with toppings, has probably been around since the Greeks and Romans, and many regions developed their own versions. However, it is the pizza of Naples that has come to be regarded as the true pizza. The first Neapolitan pizzas were white, made with garlic, lard, salt and anchovies. It was the tomato that was to transform pizza and the Neapolitans were the first Europeans to embrace this new fruit, growing them from seeds brought from the New World. The first tomato pizza was probably the classic marinara.

By the mid-nineteenth century, pizzerias had opened in Naples and wandering vendors sold slices to people on the streets. A way of life was born for the Neapolitans and their pizza began to achieve wider notoriety, with visitors venturing into poor neighbourhoods to sample this new food. When Queen Margherita visited in 1889, she too wanted to try the famous pizza. A pizzaiolo named Raffaele Esposito was summoned and he created a pizza of mozzarella, tomatoes and basil based on the colours of the Italian flag – later to be named after the Queen.

Pizza is the classic fast food and today in Naples traditional round pizzas are baked to order, then folded into quarters and wrapped in paper to take away. Elsewhere, it is more usual to find pizza a taglio, pizza that has been baked in a large tray and sold by the slice. Probably originating in Rome, pizza a taglio can be ordered by weight in many places and reheated as a snack or lunch.

Associazione Vera Pizza Napoletana (The True Neapolitan Pizza Association) has been set up to safeguard the pizza. Their guidelines include that the dough must be made only from flour, yeast, salt and water and it must not be worked by machine. Pizzas are to be cooked directly on the floor of a brick or stone-lined wood-fired oven and the temperature must exceed 400°C (750°F). The cornicione (border) must be high and soft and the whole crust not too crisp. A pizza should take only 2 minutes to cook and should be brown and crisp with the ingredients melted together.

Emigrating Neapolitans took pizza with them to America and, by the 1950s, pizza could probably be found more easily in America than in the north of Italy. When the rest of Italy did take to pizza, they adapted it to their own tastes: the Roman pizza has more topping, is thinner and crisper and does not have a cornicione.

Chapter 6

Pasta, Rice and Polenta

Pasta in many shapes and sizes is served with a variety of sauces and there are numerous regional specialities. For creamy, comfort food, there's risotto, while polenta is often served as an accompaniment to sauces and rich stews.

ROMA

LASAGNE AL FORNO
Oven-baked Lasagne

MEAT SAUCE
30 g (1 oz) butter
1 onion, finely chopped
1 small carrot, finely chopped
1/2 celery stalk, finely chopped
1 garlic clove, crushed
120 g (4 oz) pancetta, sliced
500 g (1 lb 2 oz) minced (ground) beef
1/4 teaspoon dried oregano
pinch of ground nutmeg
90 g (3 oz) chicken livers, trimmed and finely chopped
80 ml (3 fl oz/1/3 cup) dry vermouth or dry white wine

330 ml (12 fl oz/1 1/3 cups) beef stock
1 tablespoon tomato paste (concentrated purée)
2 tablespoons thick (double/heavy) cream
1 egg, beaten

1 quantity béchamel sauce (page 244)
125 ml (4 fl oz/1/2 cup) thick (double/heavy) cream
100 g (4 oz) fresh lasagne verde or 6 sheets
   dried lasagne
150 g (6 oz/1 cup) grated mozzarella cheese
65 g (2 oz/2/3 cup) grated Parmesan cheese

To make the meat sauce, heat the butter in a large frying pan and add the chopped vegetables, garlic and pancetta. Cook over moderately low heat for 5–6 minutes, or until softened and lightly golden. Add the minced beef, increase the heat a little and cook for 8 minutes, or until coloured but not browned, stirring to break up the lumps. Add the oregano and nutmeg and season well.

Add the chicken livers and cook until they change colour. Pour in the vermouth, increase the heat and cook until it has evaporated. Add the stock and tomato paste and simmer for 2 hours. Add a little hot water, if necessary, during this time to keep the mixture moist, but towards the end let all the liquid be absorbed. Stir in the cream and remove from the heat. Leave to cool for 15 minutes, then stir in the egg.

Put the béchamel sauce in a saucepan, heat gently and stir in the cream. Remove from the heat and cool slightly.

Preheat the oven to 180°C (350°F/Gas 4). Grease a 22 x 15 x 7 cm (9 x 6 x 2 3/4 in) ovenproof dish.

If you are using fresh pasta, cut it into manageable sheets and cook in batches in a large saucepan of boiling salted water until al dente. Scoop out each batch with a slotted spoon as it is done and drop into a bowl of cold water. Spread the sheets out in a single layer on a tea towel, turning them over once to dry each side. Trim away any torn edges.

Spread half the meat sauce in the dish. Scatter with half the grated mozzarella, then cover with a slightly overlapping layer of pasta sheets. Spread half the béchamel over this and sprinkle with half the Parmesan. Repeat the layers, finishing with a layer of béchamel and Parmesan.

Bake for about 40 minutes, or until golden brown and leave to rest for 10 minutes before serving.

SERVES 6

Pasta in Brodo

Pasta in Broth

Different pastas can be served in brodo (broth). Tortellini in brodo is often served as the primo piatto at celebrations. At other times, any plainer pasta is used with vegetables for a simple soup.

BROTH
2 tablespoons olive oil
1 large onion, chopped
2 carrots, chopped
1 celery stalk, chopped
1.5 kg (3 lb 5 oz) chicken bones
4 large garlic cloves, unpeeled
1 bay leaf

small bunch of parsley stalks and sprigs of thyme
1 large wine glass of red or white wine

24 fresh tortellini or some large ravioli (wild mushroom or meat stuffings are particularly good)
grated Parmesan cheese
3 tablespoons roughly chopped flat-leaf (Italian) parsley

To make the broth, heat the olive oil in a saucepan and lightly brown the onion, carrot and celery. Add the chicken bones and lightly brown (this will give a good flavour to your broth). Add the garlic, herbs and wine, cook for a few minutes to reduce, then add enough water to completely cover the bones. Bring slowly to the boil, skimming the top several times to get rid of any scum that rises to the surface of the broth.

Gently simmer the broth for at least 1 hour. Strain through a fine sieve, pour the broth back into a saucepan and return to the heat. Cook until the broth has reduced a little (this will give it a more concentrated, gutsy flavour). Taste the broth and remove from the heat when you feel the flavour is strong enough. This should produce about 1.35 litres (47 fl oz/5½ cups) of flavoursome broth.

For a clearer broth, leave to chill in the refrigerator overnight, then scrape all of the fat and sediment from the surface and pour off the broth, leaving the sediment behind. (Up to this point, the broth can be made in advance and can be frozen for a few months – any longer and the flavour will start to diminish.)

Cook the pasta in a large saucepan of boiling salted water until al dente. Meanwhile, heat the broth in another saucepan (don't be tempted to cook the pasta in the broth – the semolina used to prevent home-made pasta sticking can spoil the flavour). Drain the pasta well and add to the heated broth. Remove from the heat and leave to infuse for a couple of minutes, then spoon the pasta into bowls and pour over the broth. Sprinkle with Parmesan and the parsley to serve.

SERVES 6

RISOTTO ALLA MILANESE

Milanese Risotto

Milanese risotto, the classic accompaniment to osso buco, takes its brilliant yellow colour from saffron and its rich flavour from beef marrow. If beef marrow is hard to find, you can use a fatty piece of lardo, prosciutto or pancetta, finely chopped.

185 ml (6 fl oz/¾ cup) dry white vermouth or white wine
large pinch of saffron threads
1.5 litres (52 fl oz/6 cups) chicken stock
100 g (4 oz) butter
75 g (3 oz) beef marrow

1 large onion, finely chopped
1 garlic clove, crushed
360 g (12 oz/1⅔ cups) risotto rice (arborio, vialone nano or carnaroli)
50 g (2 oz/½ cup) grated Parmesan cheese

Put the vermouth in a bowl, add the saffron and leave to soak. Put the stock in a saucepan, bring to the boil and then maintain at a low simmer.

Melt the butter and beef marrow in a large wide heavy-based saucepan. Add the onion and garlic and cook until softened but not browned. Add the rice and reduce the heat to low. Season and stir briefly to thoroughly coat the rice. Add the vermouth and saffron to the rice. Increase the heat and cook, stirring, until all the liquid has been absorbed.

Stir in a ladleful of the simmering stock and cook over moderate heat, stirring continuously. When all of the stock has been absorbed, stir in another ladleful. Continue like this for about 20 minutes, until all the stock has been added and the rice is al dente. (You may not need to use all the stock, or you may need a little extra – every risotto will be slightly different.)

Stir in a handful of Parmesan and serve the rest on the side for people to help themselves.

SERVES 6 AS A SIDE DISH

POLENTA AI FUNGHI

Polenta with Wild Mushrooms

Polenta, made from coarse-ground corn, was known as the food of the poor in Roman times. Today, especially among Italians living abroad, it has a wide and loving audience. Sometimes polenta is so fine it is almost white; more often it is golden yellow.

POLENTA
1 tablespoon salt
300 g (11 oz/2 cups) coarse-grain polenta
50 g (2 oz) butter
75 g (3 oz/¾ cup) grated Parmesan cheese

60 ml (2 fl oz/¼ cup) olive oil
400 g (14 oz) selection of wild mushrooms, particularly fresh porcini, sliced if large, or chestnut mushrooms
2 garlic cloves, crushed
1 tablespoon chopped thyme
150 g (6 oz) mascarpone cheese

Bring 1.5 litres (52 fl oz/6 cups) water to the boil in a heavy-based saucepan and add the salt. Add the polenta in a gentle stream, whisking or stirring vigorously as you pour it in. Reduce the heat immediately so that the water is simmering. Stir continuously for the first 30 seconds to avoid any lumps appearing. Once you have stirred well at the beginning you can leave the polenta to mildly bubble away, stirring every few minutes to prevent it from sticking. Cook for 40 minutes.

Meanwhile, prepare the mushrooms. Heat the olive oil in a large saucepan or frying pan. When the oil is hot, add enough mushrooms to cover the base of the pan and cook over high heat, stirring often. Season with salt and pepper. Sometimes the mushrooms can become watery when cooked: just keep cooking until all the liquid has evaporated. Add a little of the garlic at the last minute to prevent it burning and then add a little thyme. Remove this batch of mushrooms from the pan and repeat the process until they are all cooked. Return all the mushrooms to the pan (if the polenta isn't cooked, leave the mushrooms in the pan and then reheat gently). Add the mascarpone and let it melt into the mushrooms.

Add the butter and 50 g (2 oz/½ cup) of the Parmesan to the cooked polenta and season with pepper. Spoon the polenta onto plates and then spoon the mushrooms on top. Sprinkle with the remaining Parmesan and serve immediately.

SERVES 6

Spaghetti alla Puttanesca

'Ladies of the Night' Pasta

Legend has it that this dish was so called because it was considered quick and easy enough for prostitutes to prepare between clients.

4 tablespoons olive oil
1 small onion, finely chopped
2 garlic cloves, thinly sliced
1 small red chilli, seeded and sliced
6 anchovy fillets, finely chopped
400 g (14 oz) tin chopped tomatoes

1 tablespoon finely chopped oregano, or ¼ teaspoon dried oregano
100 g (4 oz) pitted black olives, halved
1 tablespoon capers, chopped if large
400 g (14 oz) spaghetti

Heat the olive oil in a large saucepan and add the onion, garlic and chilli. Fry gently for 6 minutes, or until the onion is soft. Add the anchovies and cook, stirring, until well mixed. Add the tomatoes, oregano, olives and capers and bring to the boil. Reduce the heat, then season and leave to simmer.

Meanwhile, cook the pasta in a large saucepan of boiling salted water until al dente. Drain, toss well with the sauce and serve at once.

PICTURE ON PAGE 168

SERVES 4

Tagliatelle alle Noci

Tagliatelle with Walnut Sauce

200 g (7 oz/2 cups) shelled walnuts
20 g (1 oz) roughly chopped flat-leaf (Italian) parsley
50 g (2 oz) butter
185 ml (6 fl oz/¾ cup) extra virgin olive oil

1 garlic clove, crushed
35 g (1 oz/⅓ cup) grated Parmesan cheese
80 ml (3 fl oz/⅓ cup) thick (double/heavy) cream
400 g (14 oz) tagliatelle

Lightly toast the walnuts in a dry frying pan over moderately high heat for 2 minutes, or until just browned. Set aside to cool for 5 minutes.

Put the walnuts and chopped parsley in a food processor and blend until finely chopped. Add the butter and mix together.

Gradually pour in the olive oil in a steady stream with the motor running. Add the garlic, Parmesan and cream. Season with salt and black pepper.

Cook the pasta in a large saucepan of boiling salted water until al dente. Drain, then toss through the sauce to serve.

SERVES 4

'Ladies of the Night' Pasta (recipe on page 167)

Ravioli

Ravioli

FILLING
30 g (1 oz) butter
½ small onion, finely chopped
2 garlic cloves, crushed
90 g (3 oz) prosciutto, finely chopped
125 g (5 oz) finely minced (ground) pork
125 g (5 oz) finely minced (ground) veal
½ teaspoon finely chopped fresh oregano,
   or ⅛ teaspoon dried oregano

1 teaspoon paprika
2 teaspoons tomato paste (concentrated purée)
125 ml (4 fl oz/½ cup) chicken stock
2 egg yolks

1 quantity pasta (page 242), rolled out
semolina
1 egg, beaten

To make the filling, heat the butter in a frying pan over moderately low heat. Cook the onion, garlic and prosciutto for 5–6 minutes without browning. Add the pork and veal, increase the heat and brown lightly, breaking up the lumps. Add the oregano and paprika, season well and stir in the tomato paste and chicken stock.

Cover the pan and cook for 50 minutes. Uncover, increase the heat and cook for another 10 minutes until the filling is quite dry. Cool, then chop to get rid of any lumps. Stir in the egg yolks.

To make the ravioli, divide the rolled out pasta into four sheets: two 30 x 20 cm (12 x 8 in) sheets and two slightly larger. Dust a work surface with semolina and lay out one of the smaller sheets (keep the rest of the pasta covered with a damp tea towel to prevent it drying out). Lightly score the pasta sheet into 24 squares. Place a scant teaspoon of filling in the centre of each square and flatten it slightly with the back of the spoon.

Brush the beaten egg along the score lines around the filling. Take one of the larger pasta sheets and cover the filling, starting at one end. Match the edges and press the top sheet onto the beaten egg as you go. Avoid stretching the top sheet, rather let it settle into place. Run your finger firmly around the filling and along the cutting lines to seal well. Use a pastry wheel or a sharp knife to cut into 24 ravioli squares.

(If you are not using the ravioli immediately, place them, well spaced out, on baking paper dusted with cornmeal and cover with a tea towel. They can be left for 1–2 hours before cooking – don't refrigerate or they will become damp.)

Cook the ravioli, in several small batches, in a large saucepan of boiling salted water until they are al dente. Remove and drain with a slotted spoon. Serve on their own or with melted butter, a drizzle of olive oil or grated Parmesan.

SERVES 4

Pasta con Fagioli
Pasta with Borlotti Beans

200 g (7 oz/1 cup) dried borlotti beans
2 tablespoons olive oil
100 g (4 oz) pancetta, diced
1 celery stalk, chopped
1 onion, finely chopped
1 carrot, diced
1 garlic clove, crushed

3 tablespoons chopped flat-leaf (Italian) parsley
1 bay leaf
400 g (14 oz) tin chopped tomatoes, drained
1.5 litres (52 fl oz/6 cups) vegetable stock
150 g (6 oz) ditalini or macaroni
drizzle of extra virgin olive oil
grated Parmesan cheese

Place the beans in a large saucepan, cover with cold water and soak overnight. Drain and rinse.

Heat the olive oil in a large saucepan and add the pancetta, celery, onion, carrot and garlic and cook over moderately low heat for 5 minutes, or until golden. Season with black pepper. Add the parsley, bay leaf, tomatoes, stock and soaked borlotti beans and bring slowly to the boil. Reduce the heat and simmer for 1–1½ hours, or until the borlotti beans are tender, adding a little boiling water every so often to maintain the level.

Add the pasta and simmer for about 6 minutes, or until the pasta is just al dente. Remove from the heat and leave to rest for 10 minutes. Serve warm with a drizzle of extra virgin olive oil over each bowl. Serve the Parmesan separately.

PICTURE ON OPPOSITE PAGE

SERVES 4

Spaghettini Aglio e Olio
Garlic and Olive Oil Spaghettini

400 g (14 oz) spaghettini
80 ml (3 fl oz/⅓ cup) olive oil
5 garlic cloves, crushed

pinch of dried chilli flakes
2 tablespoons finely chopped flat-leaf (Italian) parsley
grated pecorino cheese

Cook the spaghettini in a large saucepan of boiling salted water until al dente.

Meanwhile, heat the oil in a large frying pan over very low heat. Add the garlic and chilli flakes and gently fry for about 2 minutes, or until the garlic has softened but not browned. Remove the frying pan from the heat.

Lightly drain the spaghettini. Don't shake it dry in the colander, as you need it to retain a little of the cooking water. Return the frying pan to the heat, add the spaghettini and parsley and toss to coat. Taste for seasoning and serve at once with the grated pecorino.

SERVES 4

Gnocchi con Pancetta e Salvia

Potato Gnocchi with Pancetta and Sage

When cooking the potatoes for gnocchi you want to keep them as dry as possible – too much moisture will result in a heavy dough. Floury potatoes have a low moisture content and baking the potatoes in their skins keeps them drier than boiling.

GNOCCHI

1 kg (2 lb 4 oz) floury potatoes, unpeeled
2 egg yolks
2 tablespoons grated Parmesan cheese
125–185 g (5–7 oz/1–1½ cups) plain
  (all-purpose) flour

SAUCE

1 tablespoon butter
75 g (3 oz) pancetta or bacon, cut into thin strips
8 very small sage or basil leaves
125 ml (4 fl oz/½ cup) thick (double/heavy) cream
50 g (2 oz/½ cup) grated Parmesan cheese

Preheat the oven to 180°C (350°F/Gas 4). Prick the potatoes all over, then bake for 1 hour, or until tender. Leave to cool for 15 minutes, then peel and mash, or put through a ricer or a food mill (do not use a blender or food processor).

Mix in the egg yolks and Parmesan, then gradually stir in the flour. When the mixture gets too dry to use a spoon, work it with your hands. Once a loose dough forms, transfer to a lightly floured surface and knead gently. Work in enough extra flour to give a soft, pliable dough that is damp to the touch but not sticky.

Divide the dough into six even portions. Working with one portion at a time, roll out on the floured surface to make a rope about 1.5 cm (⅝ in) thick. Cut the rope into 1.5 cm (⅝ in) lengths. Take a piece of dough and press your finger into it to form a concave shape, then roll the outer surface over the tines of a fork to make deep ridges. Fold the outer lips in towards each other to make a hollow in the middle. Continue making gnocchi with the remaining dough.

Bring a large saucepan of salted water to the boil. Add the gnocchi in batches, about 20 at a time. Stir, then return to the boil. Cook for 1–2 minutes, or until the gnocchi rise to the surface. Remove with a slotted spoon, drain and put in a greased shallow casserole or baking tray. Preheat the oven to 200°C (400°F/Gas 6).

To make the sauce, melt the butter in a small frying pan. Fry the pancetta until crisp, then stir in the sage leaves and cream. Season and simmer for 10 minutes, or until thickened.

Pour the warm sauce over the gnocchi, then toss gently and sprinkle the Parmesan on top. Bake for 10–15 minutes, or until the Parmesan melts and turns golden. Serve hot.

SERVES 4

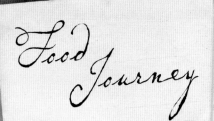

Food Journey

PASTA

Pasta was originally a southern Italian, particularly Sicilian, dish, with the first pasta industry located in Naples to take advantage of its pure water, local grain and abundant sunshine.

It was Mussolini who encouraged the cultivation of wheat, and therefore pasta, to other areas of Italy, and emigrating Italians who made it famous throughout the world. Nowadays, northern Italy tends to favour fresh egg and filled pastas (pasta fresca), often with rich meat or cream sauces or sometimes with just melted butter and Parmesan. Emilia-Romagna in the North rivals Naples as the centre of pasta production, with fresh pasta made daily. The South specializes in dried durum wheat semolina pasta made without egg (pasta secca). The hard durum wheat is needed to form the pasta into shapes and to maintain its al dente consistency. This dried pasta is usually eaten with less rich and vegetable sauces. In Italy, pasta tends to be eaten as a primo piatti (first course) rather than as a main course, and is always cooked fresh to order.

Different pastas are crafted to complement certain sauces. Shapes are often available as lisci (smooth) and rigati (ridged) and should be served with just enough sauce to coat them. The drained cooking water from the pasta can be added to the sauce if it is too thick.

Small pasta shapes (such as alfabeto, ditalini, orzo and stelline), known as pastina, are usually added to soups. There are many different shapes, ranging from letters and numbers to stars, rings and tiny pasta shells.

Long pastas (such as spaghetti, bucatini, linguine, ziti and trenette) are best eaten with fine-textured sauces such as pesto, tomato sauce or a meat ragù that will cling to their lengths. They are also used in pasticcios.

Pasta ribbons (such as tagliatelle and fettuccine) should be served with simple, fresh flavourings such as truffles or with creamy mushroom or ham sauces. When yellow and green ribbons are served together they are known as 'straw and hay'.

Pasta shapes (such as orecchiette, lumache and fusilli) are served with thicker, chunkier sauces, which are trapped by their shape. Pasta shapes also go well with sauces that have pieces of sausage, seafood or vegetable in them or with thicker soup-like dishes such as pasta e fagioli.

Stuffed pastas (such as cappelletti, tortelli and ravioli) have flavoured fillings of meat, spinach or pumpkin, and go well with simple sauces of butter and sage, fresh tomato sauce or in a pasta in brodo.

RISOTTO NERO

Squid Ink Risotto

You can sometimes buy the ink sac of the squid from your fishmonger, although most are lost or burst by the time the squid reaches the shop. The little sachets of ink are more easily found.

2 medium-sized squid
1 litre (35 fl oz/4 cups) fish stock
100 g (4 oz) butter
1 red onion, finely chopped
2 garlic cloves, crushed
360 g (12 oz/1²/₃ cups) risotto rice (arborio, vialone nano or carnaroli)

3 sachets of squid or cuttlefish ink, or the ink sac of a large cuttlefish
170 ml (6 fl oz/²/₃ cup) white wine
2 teaspoons olive oil

Prepare the squid by pulling out the heads and tentacles from the bodies along with any innards. Cut the heads off below the eyes, leaving just the tentacles. Discard the heads and set the tentacles aside. Rinse the bodies, pulling out the transparent quills. Finely chop the bodies.

Put the stock in a saucepan, bring to the boil and then maintain at a low simmer.

Heat the butter in a large, wide heavy-based saucepan. Cook the onion until softened but not browned. Increase the heat and add the chopped squid. Cook for 3–5 minutes, or until the squid turns opaque. Add the garlic and stir briefly. Add the rice and reduce the heat to low. Season and stir briefly to thoroughly coat the rice.

Squeeze out the ink from the sachets and add to the rice with the wine. Increase the heat and stir until all the liquid has been absorbed.

Stir in a ladleful of the simmering stock and cook over moderate heat, stirring continuously. When the stock has been absorbed, add another ladleful. Continue like this for about 20 minutes, until all the stock has been added and the rice is al dente. (You may not need to use all of the stock, or you may need to add a little extra – every risotto will be slightly different.)

Heat the olive oil in a frying pan and quickly fry the squid tentacles. Garnish the risotto with the tentacles and serve immediately.

SERVES 6 AS A STARTER

Pasticcio di Tortellini, Broccoli e Ricotta
Pasticcio of Tortellini, Broccoli and Ricotta

FILLING
650 g (1 lb 7 oz) ricotta cheese
pinch of ground nutmeg
100 g (4 oz/1 cup) grated Parmesan cheese
1 egg

600 g (1 lb 5 oz) broccoli, trimmed into florets
500 g (1 lb 2 oz) cheese-filled tortellini

3 eggs
1 quantity béchamel sauce (page 244)
1½ tablespoons tomato paste (concentrated purée)
150 g (6 oz/1 cup) grated mozzarella cheese
4 tablespoons grated Parmesan cheese

To make the filling, mash the ricotta cheese with a fork, or pass through a food mill (do not use a blender or food processor). Mix in the nutmeg and season with salt and pepper. Add the grated Parmesan, then mix in the egg. Set aside.

Preheat the oven to 180°C (350°F/Gas 4) and grease a large deep casserole dish. Bring a large saucepan of water to the boil. Add the broccoli florets and a teaspoon of salt and simmer for 3 minutes. Remove the broccoli with a slotted spoon and set aside. Stir the tortellini into the boiling water and then gently lower in the eggs. Cook until the pasta is al dente, drain and rinse under cold water. Take out the eggs after about 6 minutes when they are hard-boiled, remove the eggshells and slice thinly.

Put half of the béchamel sauce into a large bowl and stir in the tomato paste. Add the tortellini and toss to coat. Pour half of the tortellini mixture into the casserole dish. Spread half of the ricotta filling over it, then top with half the egg slices. Layer all the broccoli on top of this, pressing it in firmly, then spoon the remaining plain béchamel sauce over the top. Sprinkle with the mozzarella. Finish with a final layer of tortellini, the remaining egg slices and finally the rest of the ricotta filling.

Sprinkle the Parmesan over the top and bake for 30–40 minutes. Remove from the oven and allow to rest for 10 minutes before serving.

SERVES 6

PASTA PRIMAVERA

Fresh Vegetable Pasta

Pasta (meaning 'dough' in Italian, from the same root as 'pastry' and the French 'pâte') has a long history and was probably enjoyed by both the ancient Greeks and Etruscans. This favourite sauce, with its fresh young vegetables, heralds the arrival of springtime.

120 g (4 oz) broad (fava) beans, fresh or frozen
150 g (6 oz) asparagus, cut into short lengths
350 g (12 oz) fresh tagliatelle
100 g (4 oz) French beans, cut into short lengths
120 g (4 oz) peas, fresh or frozen

30 g (1 oz) butter
1 small fennel bulb, thinly sliced
375 ml (13 fl oz/1½ cups) thick (double/heavy) cream
2 tablespoons grated Parmesan cheese, plus extra
  to serve

Bring a large saucepan of water to the boil. Add 1 teaspoon of salt, the broad beans and asparagus and simmer for 3 minutes.

Remove the vegetables with a slotted spoon and set aside. Add the pasta to the saucepan and, when it has softened, stir in the French beans and peas (if you're using frozen peas add them a few minutes later). Cook for about 4 minutes, or until the pasta is al dente.

Meanwhile, heat the butter in a large frying pan. Add the fennel and cook over moderately low heat without browning for 5 minutes. Add the cream, season and cook at a low simmer.

Peel the skins from the broad beans. Drain the pasta, French beans and peas and add to the cream mixture. Add 2 tablespoons of Parmesan and the broad beans and asparagus. Toss lightly to coat. Serve immediately, with extra Parmesan.

SERVES 4

Tagliatelle al Ragù

Tagliatelle with Ragù

Spaghetti bolognese is one of the most popular and well-known Italian dishes around the world. However, the Italians themselves would never dream of serving their traditional bolognese sauce on spaghetti – tagliatelle is the usual accompaniment.

60 g (2 oz) butter
1 onion, finely chopped
1 celery stalk, finely chopped
1 carrot, finely chopped
90 g (3 oz) pancetta or bacon, finely chopped
225 g (8 oz) minced (ground) beef
225 g (8 oz) minced (ground) pork
2 sprigs of oregano, chopped, or ¼ teaspoon
  dried oregano
pinch of ground nutmeg
120 g (4 oz) chicken livers, trimmed and finely chopped
125 ml (4 fl oz/½ cup) dry white wine
185 ml (6 fl oz/¾ cup) milk
400 g (14 oz) tin chopped tomatoes
250 ml (9 fl oz/1 cup) beef stock
400 g (14 oz) tagliatelle
grated Parmesan cheese

Heat the butter in a saucepan and add the onion, celery, carrot and pancetta. Cook over moderate heat for 6–8 minutes, stirring from time to time.

Add the beef, pork and oregano to the saucepan. Season with salt and pepper and the nutmeg. Cook for about 5 minutes, or until the mince has changed colour but not browned. Add the chicken liver and cook until it changes colour.

Pour in the wine, increase the heat and boil over high heat for 2–3 minutes, or until the wine has been absorbed. Stir in 125 ml (4 fl oz/½ cup) of the milk, then reduce the heat and simmer for 10 minutes. Add the tomatoes and half the stock, partially cover the pan and leave to simmer gently over very low heat for 3 hours. Add more of the stock as it is needed to keep the sauce moist.

Meanwhile, cook the pasta in a large saucepan of boiling salted water until al dente.

Stir the remaining milk into the sauce 5 minutes before serving. Taste the sauce for seasoning, then drain the tagliatelle, toss with the sauce and serve with grated Parmesan.

SERVES 4

Polenta ai Quattro Formaggi

Baked Polenta with Four Cheeses

If you have time, use 'proper' polenta instead of the quick-cook variety. It might seem labour intensive, as you have to stir constantly, but the flavour is better. In Italy they solve the problem by having 'self-stirring' polenta pans with a revolving spoon.

POLENTA
1 tablespoon salt
300 g (11 oz/2 cups) coarse-grain polenta
75 g (3 oz) butter

TOMATO SAUCE
3 tablespoons olive oil
2 garlic cloves, thinly sliced

15 g (½ oz) rosemary or thyme, roughly chopped
800 g (1 lb 12 oz) tin tomatoes
200 g (7 oz) Gorgonzola, cubed
250 g (9 oz) Taleggio cheese, cubed
250 g (9 oz) mascarpone cheese
100 g (4 oz/1 cup) grated Parmesan cheese

Bring 1.5 litres (52 fl oz/6 cups) water to the boil in a heavy-based saucepan and add the salt. Add the polenta to the pan in a gentle stream, whisking or stirring vigorously as you pour it in. Reduce the heat immediately so that the water is simmering. Stir continuously for the first 30 seconds to avoid any lumps appearing – the more you stir, the better the texture will be. Once you have stirred well at the beginning you can leave the polenta to bubble away, stirring it every few minutes to prevent it sticking. Cook for 40 minutes. Add the butter and mix well.

Pour the polenta into a shallow casserole or baking tray about 5 cm (2 in) deep (you want the polenta to come no more than halfway up the side of the dish). Leave to cool completely.

To make the tomato sauce, heat the olive oil in a saucepan and cook the garlic gently until light brown. Add half the rosemary or thyme and then the tomatoes. Season with salt and pepper and cook gently, stirring occasionally, until reduced to a thick sauce.

Preheat the oven to 180°C (350°F/Gas 4). Turn the polenta out of the dish and onto a board, then slice it horizontally in two. Pour half the tomato sauce into the bottom of the empty dish. Place the bottom slice of the polenta on top of the sauce and season. Scatter the Gorgonzola and Taleggio over the top. Dot the mascarpone over the polenta with a teaspoon, and sprinkle with half the Parmesan and the remaining herbs.

Put the other layer of polenta on top and pour over the remaining tomato sauce. Sprinkle with the remaining Parmesan and bake for 30 minutes. Leave to rest for 10 minutes before serving with a simple rocket (arugula) salad.

SERVES 6

SPAGHETTI CARBONARA

Egg and Bacon Spaghetti

400 g (14 oz) spaghetti
2 eggs
2 egg yolks
65 g (2 oz/^{2}/$_3$ cup) grated Parmesan cheese,
 plus extra for serving

2 tablespoons olive oil
30 g (1 oz) butter
2 garlic cloves
200 g (7 oz) pancetta, cut into small strips

Cook the pasta in a large saucepan of boiling salted water until al dente. Meanwhile, mix the eggs, egg yolks and Parmesan together in a bowl and season lightly.

Heat the oil and butter in a large frying pan. Bruise the garlic cloves with the back of a knife and add to the pan with the pancetta. Cook over moderate heat until the pancetta is crisp, discarding the garlic when it becomes golden.

Drain the pasta, add to the frying pan and toss well. Remove from the heat and stir in the egg mixture. Serve immediately, with Parmesan.

PICTURE ON OPPOSITE PAGE

SERVES 4

RISI E BISI

Peas and Rice

The consistency of risi e bisi is thick, halfway between a risotto and a soup in texture and appearance. You can cook it thin enough to eat with a spoon, or thick enough to use a fork. Some versions are very simple and do not even include pancetta.

1.5 litres (52 fl oz/6 cups) chicken stock
2 teaspoons olive oil
40 g (1½ oz) butter
85 g (3 oz) pancetta, diced
1 small onion, finely chopped

2 tablespoons chopped flat-leaf (Italian) parsley
390 g (14 oz/2½ cups) shelled young peas
200 g (7 oz) risotto rice (arborio, vialone nano
 or carnaroli)
50 g (2 oz/½ cup) grated Parmesan cheese

Put the stock in a saucepan and bring to the boil, then maintain at a low simmer. Heat the olive oil and half the butter in a large, wide heavy-based saucepan over low heat. Cook the pancetta and onion for 5 minutes, or until soft. Add the parsley, peas and 2 ladlefuls of stock. Simmer for 7 minutes.

Add the rice and remaining stock. Simmer until the rice is al dente and most of the stock has been absorbed. Stir in the remaining butter and the Parmesan, season and serve.

SERVES 4

GNOCCHI ALLA ROMANA

Roman Gnocchi

These gnocchi can be prepared a day or two in advance, wrapped and stored in the refrigerator in the slab form or as circles. Roman gnocchi are made with semolina and are quite different from the more well-known potato gnocchi.

45 g (1½ oz) unsalted butter, melted
35 g (1 oz/⅓ cup) grated Parmesan cheese
3 egg yolks
1 litre (32 fl oz/4 cups) milk
pinch of ground nutmeg
200 g (7 oz/1⅔ cups) semolina flour

TOPPING
40 g (1½ oz) butter, melted
80 ml (3 fl oz/⅓ cup) thick (double/heavy) cream
35 g (1 oz/⅓ cup) grated Parmesan cheese

Line a 30 x 25 cm (12 x 10 in) swiss roll tin with baking paper. Beat together the butter, Parmesan and egg yolks and season lightly. Set aside.

Heat the milk in a large saucepan. Add the nutmeg and season with salt and pepper. When the milk is just boiling, pour in the semolina in a steady stream, stirring as you pour. Reduce the heat and continue to cook, stirring, for 10–12 minutes, or until all the milk has been absorbed and the mixture pulls away from the side of the pan in one mass. Remove the pan from the heat and beat in the egg yolk mixture. When smooth, spoon quickly into the swiss roll tin. Smooth the surface using a knife dipped in cold water. Set aside to cool.

Preheat the oven to 180°C (350°F/Gas 4) and grease a 25 x 18 cm (10 x 7 in) shallow casserole or baking tray.

Lift the semolina slab out of the tin and peel off the paper. Cut circles from the semolina, using a 4 cm (1½ in) biscuit cutter dipped in water. Arrange the circles, slightly overlapping, in the casserole.

To make the topping, blend together the butter and cream. Pour this over the gnocchi and sprinkle the Parmesan on top. Bake for 25–30 minutes, or until golden. Serve at once.

SERVES 4

A biscuit cutter gives a good clean edge to the gnocchi. If you don't have one, use an upturned glass or teacup instead.

SPAGHETTI MARINARA

Spaghetti with Prawns, Clams and Scallops

Seafood pasta in many restaurants around the world is erroneously termed marinara. Marinara is traditionally the sauce made by fishermen (or their wives), to which the day's catch would be added. So the name, in fact, refers to the sauce, not the seafood.

250 ml (9 fl oz/1 cup) dry white wine
pinch of saffron threads
1 kg (2 lb 4 oz) clams (vongole)
4 baby octopus
200 g (7 oz) small squid tubes
500 g (1 lb 2 oz) prawns (shrimp)
6 tomatoes

400 g (14 oz) spaghetti
4 tablespoons olive oil
3 garlic cloves, crushed
8–10 scallops, cleaned
6 tablespoons chopped flat-leaf (Italian)
   parsley
lemon wedges

Put the wine and saffron in a bowl and leave to infuse. Clean the clams by scrubbing thoroughly and scraping off any barnacles. Rinse well under running water and discard any that are broken or open and don't close when tapped on the bench. Place the clams in a large saucepan with 185 ml (6 fl oz/¾ cup) water. Cover the pan and cook over high heat for 1–2 minutes, or until the clams open (discard any that stay closed after that time). Drain, reserving the liquid. Remove the clams from their shells and set aside.

Clean the octopus by slitting the head and pulling out the innards. Cut out the eyes and hard beak and rinse. Lie the squid out flat, skin-side up, and score a crisscross pattern in the flesh, being careful not to cut all the way through. Slice diagonally into 2 x 4 cm (¾ x 1½ in) strips. Peel and devein the prawns.

Score a cross in the top of each tomato, plunge them into boiling water for 20 seconds, then drain and peel the skin away from the cross. Core and chop. Cook the pasta in a large saucepan of boiling salted water until al dente.

Meanwhile, heat the oil in a large frying pan and add the garlic and tomato. Stir over moderate heat for 10–15 seconds, then pour in the saffron-infused wine and reserved clam liquid. Season and simmer for 8–10 minutes, or until reduced by half. Add the squid, prawns and octopus and cook until the squid turns opaque. Add the scallops, clam meat and parsley and cook until the scallops turn opaque.

Drain the spaghetti and return to the pan. Add two-thirds of the sauce, toss well then transfer to a large serving platter. Spoon the remaining sauce over the top and serve with lemon wedges.

SERVES 4

CANNELLONI

Pork and Veal Cannelloni

MEAT SAUCE
3 tablespoons olive oil
1 onion, finely chopped
2 garlic cloves, crushed
120 g (4 oz) bacon, finely chopped
60 g (2 oz) button mushrooms, finely chopped
1/4 teaspoon dried basil
225 g (8 oz) minced (ground) pork
225 g (8 oz) minced (ground) veal
1 tablespoon finely chopped flat-leaf
   (Italian) parsley
200 g (7 oz) tin chopped tomatoes
250 ml (9 fl oz/1 cup) beef stock
3 tablespoons dried breadcrumbs
1 egg

TOMATO SAUCE
2 tablespoons olive oil
1 small onion, finely chopped
2 garlic cloves, crushed
2 x 400 g (14 oz) tins chopped tomatoes
1 teaspoon chopped basil

10 sheets fresh lasagne, about 17 x 12 cm (7 x 5 in)
   (the grain of the pasta should run with the width not
   the length, or the pasta will split when rolled up), or
   1 1/2 quantities pasta (page 242) rolled and cut into
   10 sheets as above
4 large slices prosciutto, cut in half
60 g (2 oz/1/2 cup) grated fontina cheese
185 ml (6 fl oz/3/4 cup) thick (double/heavy) cream
65 g (2 oz/2/3 cup) grated Parmesan cheese

To make the meat sauce, heat the oil in a frying pan and cook the onion, garlic and bacon over moderate heat for 6 minutes, or until the onion is soft and golden. Stir in the mushrooms and basil, cook for 2–3 minutes, then add the pork and veal. Cook, stirring often to break up the lumps, until the meat has changed colour. Season well, add the parsley, tomatoes and stock, partially cover the pan and simmer for 1 hour. Remove the lid and then simmer for another 30 minutes to reduce the liquid. Cool slightly, then stir in the breadcrumbs, then the egg.

To make the tomato sauce, heat the oil in a frying pan and cook the onion and garlic for 6 minutes, or until the onion has softened but not browned. Stir in the tomatoes and the basil. Add 250 ml (9 fl oz/1 cup) water and season well. Simmer for 30 minutes, or until you have a thick sauce.

Cook the lasagne in batches in a large saucepan of boiling salted water until al dente. Scoop out each batch with a slotted spoon and drop into a bowl of cold water. Spread the sheets out in a single layer on a tea towel, turning them over once to dry each side. Trim away any torn edges. (We have allowed two extra sheets of lasagne in case of tearing.)

Preheat the oven to 190°C (375°F/Gas 5). Grease a shallow 30 x 18 cm (12 x 7 in) ovenproof dish and spoon the tomato sauce over the base.

Place a half slice of prosciutto over each pasta sheet and top with a sprinkling of fontina. Spoon an eighth of the meat filling across one end of the pasta sheet. Starting from this end, roll the pasta up tightly to enclose the filling. Place the filled rolls, seam side down, in a row in the dish.

Beat together the cream and grated Parmesan and season well. Spoon over the cannelloni so that it is well covered. Bake for 20 minutes, or until lightly browned on top. Leave to rest for 10 minutes before serving.

PICTURE ON PAGE 198   SERVES 4

Pork and Veal Cannelloni (recipe on page 197)

Risotto ai Funghi
Mushroom Risotto

20 g (1 oz) dried porcini mushrooms
1 litre (32 fl oz/4 cups) vegetable or chicken stock
2 tablespoons olive oil
1 tablespoon butter
1 small onion, finely chopped
2 garlic cloves, crushed

375 g (13 oz/1¾ cups) risotto rice (arborio, vialone nano or carnaroli)
250 g (9 oz) mushrooms, sliced
pinch of ground nutmeg
50 g (2 oz/½ cup) grated Parmesan cheese
3 tablespoons finely chopped flat-leaf (Italian) parsley

Soak the porcini in 500 ml (17 fl oz/2 cups) of boiling water for 30 minutes. Drain, retaining the liquid. Chop the mushrooms and pass the liquid through a fine sieve. Put the stock in a saucepan and bring to the boil, then reduce the heat and maintain at a low simmer.

Heat the oil and butter in a large, wide heavy-based saucepan. Cook the onion and garlic until softened but not browned. Add the rice and reduce the heat to low. Season and stir to thoroughly coat the rice. Toss in the fresh mushrooms and ground nutmeg.

Season and cook, stirring, for 1–2 minutes. Add the porcini and their liquid, increase the heat and cook until the liquid has been absorbed.

Stir in a ladleful of stock and cook over moderate heat, stirring continuously. When the stock has been absorbed, stir in another ladleful. Continue like this for about 20 minutes, until all the stock has been added and the rice is al dente. (You may not need to use all the stock, or you may need a little extra.) Remove from the heat and stir in the Parmesan and parsley. Season and serve.

PICTURE ON OPPOSITE PAGE

SERVES 4

Penne all'Arrabbiata
Penne with Tomato and Chilli

2 tablespoons olive oil
2 large garlic cloves, thinly sliced
1–2 medium-sized dried chillies

800 g (1 lb 12 oz) tin tomatoes
400 g (14 oz) penne or rigatoni
1 sprig of basil, torn into pieces

Heat the oil in a saucepan over low heat. Add the garlic and chilli and cook, turning the chilli, until the garlic is light golden brown. Add the tomatoes and season with salt. Cook gently, breaking up the tomatoes with a wooden spoon, for 20–30 minutes, or until the sauce is rich and thick.

Meanwhile, cook the pasta in a large saucepan of boiling salted water until al dente. Drain.

Add the basil to the sauce and season just before serving, tossed with the pasta. Break open the chilli to release the seeds if you prefer a hotter sauce.

SERVES 4

TORTELLINI ALLA ZUCCA

Tortellini filled with Pumpkin and Sage

Legend has it that Venus, barred from heaven, sought refuge in an inn in Bologna instead. The innkeeper, filled with lust, spied on her through the keyhole, then rushed to his kitchen to create pasta in the shape of her navel – tortellini.

FILLING
900 g (2 lb) pumpkin or butternut squash,
  peeled and cubed
6 tablespoons olive oil
1 small red onion, finely chopped
90 g (3 oz/⅓ cup) ricotta cheese
1 egg yolk, beaten
25 g (1 oz/¼ cup) grated Parmesan cheese
1 teaspoon grated nutmeg
2 tablespoons chopped sage

1 quantity pasta (page 242), rolled out
1 egg
2 teaspoons milk
grated Parmesan cheese

SAGE BUTTER
250 g (9 oz) butter
10 g (½ oz/½ cup) sage leaves

To make the filling, preheat the oven to 190°C (375°F/Gas 5). Put the pumpkin in a roasting tin with half the olive oil and lots of salt and pepper. Bake for 40 minutes, or until the pumpkin is completely soft.

Meanwhile, heat the remaining oil in a saucepan and gently cook the onion until soft. Put the onion and pumpkin in a bowl, draining off any excess oil, and mash well. Leave to cool, then crumble in the ricotta. Mix in the egg yolk, Parmesan, nutmeg and sage. Season well.

To make the tortellini, cut the rolled out pasta into 8 cm (3 in) squares. Mix together the egg and milk to make an egg wash and brush lightly over the pasta just before you fill each one. Put a teaspoon of filling in the middle of each square and fold it over diagonally to make a triangle, pressing down the corners. Pinch together the two corners on the longer side.

(If you are not using the tortellini immediately, place them, well spaced out, on baking paper dusted with cornmeal and cover with a tea towel. They can be left for 1–2 hours before cooking– don't refrigerate or they will become damp.)

Cook the tortellini, in small batches, in a large saucepan of boiling salted water until al dente. Remove and drain with a slotted spoon.

To make the sage butter, melt the butter slowly with the sage and leave to infuse for at least 5 minutes. Drizzle over the tortellini and serve with a sprinkling of Parmesan.

SERVES 6

Vincisgrassi
Baked Pasta

MEAT SAUCE
40 g (1½ oz) butter
2 cotechino sausages, casings removed, chopped
800 g (1 lb 12 oz) boneless, skinless chicken thighs,
   cut into thin strips
300 g (11 oz) chicken livers, trimmed and chopped
80 ml (3 fl oz/⅓ cup) dry Marsala
185 ml (6 fl oz/¾ cup) chicken stock

MUSHROOM SAUCE
10 g (½ oz) dried porcini mushrooms
40 g (1½ oz) butter

1 onion, finely chopped
100 g (4 oz) button mushrooms, thinly sliced
pinch of ground nutmeg
1 tablespoon chicken stock

1½ quantities béchamel sauce (page 244)
100 g (4 oz) fresh lasagne or 6 sheets dried lasagne
75 g (3 oz/¾ cup) grated Parmesan cheese

To make the meat sauce, heat the butter in a large frying pan and cook the sausage meat until browned, stirring to break up any lumps. Add the chicken and lightly brown. Increase the heat, add the liver and fry quickly, stirring, until darkened. Season, pour in the Marsala and stir until almost evaporated, then add the stock. Cover, reduce the heat and simmer for 25 minutes.

To make the mushroom sauce, soak the porcini mushrooms in 80 ml (3 fl oz/⅓ cup) warm water for 30 minutes. Drain and finely chop the porcini. Heat the butter in a saucepan and soften the onion over low heat for 5–6 minutes. Add the porcini and button mushrooms and cook over high heat for 2–3 minutes. Add the nutmeg and chicken stock. Season and simmer for 8–10 minutes, or until all the liquid has evaporated.

Pour one third of the béchamel sauce into a bowl and refrigerate. Add the mushroom sauce to the remaining béchamel and mix well.

If you are using fresh pasta, cook in batches in a large saucepan of boiling salted water until al dente. Scoop out each batch with a slotted spoon and drop into a bowl of cold water. Spread the sheets out in a single layer on a tea towel, turning them over once to blot dry each side. Trim away any torn edges.

Grease a large ovenproof dish and arrange an overlapping layer of pasta in the base. Top with half of the meat sauce, then spread half of the mushroom sauce over the top. Sprinkle with one third of the grated Parmesan. Repeat the layers, then finish with a layer of pasta. Refrigerate the last of the Parmesan. Cover the vincisgrassi with plastic wrap and refrigerate for at least 6 hours.

Preheat the oven to 200°C (400°F/Gas 6). Spoon the reserved béchamel sauce over the top of the pasta and sprinkle the remaining Parmesan over this. Bake for 30 minutes, or until golden, and rest for 10 minutes before serving.

SERVES 6

Chapter 7

DESSERTS AND BAKING

*Italy is renowned for its gelati and sorbets, the tiramisù of Treviso,
the panforte of Siena and the dome-shaped zuccotto of Florence.
Desserts often showcase seasonal fruits that are simply poached or grilled.*

ZUCCOTTO

Tuscan Semifreddo

Zuccotto is a speciality of the city of Florence – its shape perhaps inspired by the rounded roof of the local duomo. Zuccotto is also a variant of Zucchetto, the name of the cardinals' skull-caps.

300 g (10½ oz) Madeira or pound cake
3 tablespoons brandy
3 tablespoons maraschino liqueur
500 ml (17 fl oz/2 cups) thick (double/heavy) cream
90 g (3 oz/¾ cup) icing (confectioners') sugar
150 g (5½ oz) dark chocolate, roughly chopped

50 g (1¾ oz) blanched almonds
25 g (1 oz) skinned hazelnuts
25 g (1 oz) candied peel, chopped
cocoa powder, to dust
icing (confectioners') sugar, to dust

Cut the cake into 1 cm (½ in) slices and then cut each slice into two triangles. Combine the brandy and maraschino and sprinkle them over the cake.

Line a 1.5 litre (52 fl oz/6 cup) bowl with a layer of plastic wrap and then with the cake slices. Arrange the slices with the narrow point of each triangle pointing into the bottom of the bowl to form a star pattern, fitting each piece against the others so you don't have any gaps. Cut smaller triangles to fit the gaps along the top and keep the rest of the cake for the top.

Whip the cream until soft peaks form and then whisk in the icing sugar until you have a stiff mixture. Add about a third of the chocolate and

the almonds, hazelnuts and candied peel. Mix together thoroughly, then fill the cake-lined bowl with half the cream mixture, making a hollow in the middle and drawing the mixture up the sides. Leave in the refrigerator.

Melt the rest of the chocolate in a heatproof bowl over a saucepan of simmering water, then fold it into the remaining cream mixture. Spoon this into the bowl and then cover the top with a layer of cake triangles, leaving no gaps. Cover the bowl with plastic wrap and then refrigerate overnight.

To serve, unmould the zuccotto and use a triangular piece of cardboard as a template to dust the top with alternating segments of cocoa and icing sugar.

SERVES 6

Far left: When filling the zuccotto, try not to disturb the pieces of cake you have arranged. The easiest way is to smooth the filling up the side.

Left: Fill the middle of the bowl with the chocolate cream, then cover the top with the remaining cake triangles.

Ficchi al Forno

Baked Figs

When not in Italy, you'll have to buy cantucci at specialist Italian grocers, although some larger supermarkets do stock them. Don't waste the rest of the packet – serve them after the figs, for dipping in after-dinner drinks like vin santo or espresso.

3 cantucci (biscotti di Prato)
1 teaspoon grated lemon zest
60 ml (2 fl oz/¼ cup) thick (double/heavy) cream

4 purple figs, ripe but firm
juice of ½ lemon
1 tablespoon soft brown sugar

Preheat the oven to 210°C (415°F/Gas 6–7) and lightly grease a shallow ovenproof dish that is large enough to hold eight fig halves. Crush the cantucci with a rolling pin. Combine the crumbs with half the lemon zest and half the cream.

Slice each fig in half lengthways and drizzle the lemon juice over the cut surfaces. Press the cantucci filling loosely onto the centres of the figs. Arrange the figs in the dish, with each stem end slightly overlapping the base of the fig in front. Pour the remaining cream over the top and sprinkle with the remaining lemon zest, then the sugar.

Bake the figs for 10 minutes, or until the sugar melts and a little syrup forms in the dish. Serve warm with a little of the syrup spooned on top, with mascarpone or whipped cream.

PICTURE ON OPPOSITE PAGE

SERVES 4

Zabaione

Zabaglione

Zabaione is one of those happy occurrences, a dish created purely by accident when, in seventeenth-century Turin, a chef poured fortified sweet wine into egg custard. In rural areas zabaione is eaten hot for breakfast.

6 egg yolks
3 tablespoons caster (superfine) sugar

125 ml (4 fl oz/½ cup) sweet Marsala
250 ml (9 fl oz/1 cup) thick (double/heavy) cream

Whisk the egg yolks and sugar together in the top of a double boiler or in a heatproof bowl set over a saucepan of simmering water. When the mixture is tepid, add the Marsala and whisk for 5 minutes, or until it has thickened.

Whip the cream until soft peaks form. Gently fold in the egg yolk mixture. Cover and refrigerate for 3–4 hours before serving.

SERVES 4

CROSTATA DI PERE
Fresh Pear Tart

PASTRY
155 g (5½ oz/1¼ cups) plain (all-purpose) flour
55 g (2 oz/¼ cup) caster (superfine) sugar
1 teaspoon grated lemon zest
60 g (2¼ oz) unsalted butter, chilled and cut
    into small cubes
1 egg yolk

MASCARPONE CREAM
125 g (4½ oz) mascarpone cheese
55 g (2 oz/¼ cup) caster (superfine) sugar
1 egg

¼ teaspoon natural vanilla extract
1 tablespoon plain (all-purpose) flour
2–3 tablespoons milk, as necessary

4 ripe pears
juice of ½ lemon
45 g (1½ oz) roasted hazelnuts, roughly chopped
1½ tablespoons caster (superfine) sugar
1 tablespoon apricot jam (jelly)
1 teaspoon pear liqueur, or other fruit-flavoured liqueur

To make the pastry, mix the flour, sugar, lemon zest and a pinch of salt in a bowl. Rub in the butter, then add the egg yolk and 2–3 teaspoons cold water and mix until the dough gathers in a loose clump. Transfer to a lightly floured surface and knead until smooth, adding more flour if needed. Chill in a plastic bag for 30 minutes.

Preheat the oven to 190°C (375°F/Gas 5) and grease a 23 cm (9 in) loose-based tart tin. Lightly dust the work surface with flour and roll the pastry out until it is large enough to fit the tin. Line the tin neatly, trimming the pastry edges with a knife. Cover the pastry with baking paper and fill with pie weights or uncooked rice or beans. Bake blind for 15 minutes, then allow to cool. Reduce the oven to 170°C (325°F/Gas 3).

To make the mascarpone cream, blend the mascarpone, sugar, egg, vanilla extract and flour together until smooth (you can also use a food processor). Add a little milk if necessary to make the cream spreadable. Spoon the mixture into the pastry shell and smooth the surface.

Peel, halve and core the pears, brushing the cut surfaces with lemon juice as you prepare each one. Arrange the pear halves like wheel spokes in the tart shell, with the wide base of each pear half to the outside. You may need to trim the last couple so they fit snugly. Place a round piece of pear in the centre. Scatter the chopped hazelnuts over the pears, then sprinkle the sugar over the top. Bake for 45 minutes, or until the filling is golden and set and the pears are soft.

Heat the jam and liqueur in a small saucepan with 2 tablespoons of water. Simmer, stirring, for 3–4 minutes until the jam has melted. Strain and brush over the pears. Serve the tart warm or at room temperature.

SERVES 6

PANNA COTTA

Vanilla Panna Cotta with Fresh Berries

Meaning 'cooked cream', this Piemontese dessert should be softly set with a yellow colour and a rich creamy texture. Don't be tempted to put any more gelatine in the mixture or your panna cotta might become rubbery.

500 ml (17 fl oz/2 cups) thick (double/heavy) cream
4 tablespoons caster (superfine) sugar
natural vanilla extract

3 sheets or 1¼ teaspoons gelatine
250 g (9 oz) fresh berries

Put the cream and sugar in a saucepan and stir over gentle heat until the sugar has dissolved. Bring to the boil, then simmer for 3 minutes, adding a few drops of vanilla extract to taste.

If using gelatine sheets, soak in cold water until they are floppy, then squeeze out any excess water. Stir the sheets into the hot cream until they are completely dissolved. If using powdered gelatine, sprinkle it onto the hot cream in an even layer and leave it to sponge for a minute, then stir it into the cream until dissolved. Pour the cream mixture into four 125 ml (4 fl oz/½ cup) dariole moulds, cover with plastic wrap and refrigerate until set.

Unmould the panna cotta by wrapping the moulds in a cloth dipped in hot water and tipping them gently onto serving plates. Serve with the berries.

PICTURE ON OPPOSITE PAGE

SERVES 4

TORTA DI CASTAGNE

Chestnut Cake

400 g (14 oz) chestnuts or 250 g (9 oz) cooked
   peeled chestnuts
5 egg yolks and 4 egg whites
200 g (7 oz) caster (superfine) sugar

100 g (3½ oz) unsalted butter, softened
1 tablespoon grated lemon zest
150 g (5½ oz/1½ cups) ground almonds
2 tablespoons plain (all-purpose) flour

Preheat the oven to 180°C (350°F/Gas 4). Grease and flour a round 20 cm (8 in) cake tin.

Cook the chestnuts in a saucepan of boiling water for 25 minutes, or until tender. Drain, then peel and, while still hot, purée and sieve. (If you are using cooked chestnuts, simply purée them.)

Whisk the egg yolks and sugar until light and fluffy. Add the butter, lemon zest, chestnut purée, ground almonds and flour and stir well. Whisk the egg whites until soft peaks form, then fold them into the chestnut mixture. Pour into the prepared tin and bake for 50–60 minutes. Cool on a wire rack and serve with whipped cream.

SERVES 8

Tiramisù

Coffee Tiramisù

Tira mi su means 'pick me up' in Italian and this is how the dessert started life – as a nourishing dish to be eaten when feeling low. You can also make a fruit version, using framboise and puréed raspberries instead of brandy and coffee.

5 eggs, separated
170 g (6 oz/¾ cup) caster (superfine) sugar
300 g (10½ oz) mascarpone cheese
250 ml (9 fl oz/1 cup) cold strong coffee

3 tablespoons brandy or sweet Marsala
36 small sponge fingers
80 g (3 oz) dark chocolate, finely grated

Beat the egg yolks with the caster sugar until the sugar has dissolved and the mixture is light and fluffy and leaves a ribbon trail when dropped from the whisk. Add the mascarpone and beat until the mixture is smooth.

Whisk the egg whites in a clean dry glass bowl, using a wire whisk or hand beaters, until soft peaks form. Fold into the mascarpone mixture.

Pour the cold coffee into a shallow dish and add the brandy. Dip enough biscuits to cover the base of a 25 cm (10 in) square dish into the coffee. The

biscuits should be fairly well soaked but not so much so that they break up. Arrange the biscuits in one tightly packed layer in the base of the dish.

Spread half the mascarpone mixture over the layer of biscuits. Add another layer of soaked biscuits and then another layer of mascarpone, smoothing the top neatly. Dust with the grated chocolate to serve. The flavours will be better developed if you make the tiramisù a few hours in advance or even the night before. If you have time to do this, don't dust with the chocolate, but cover with plastic wrap and chill. Dust with chocolate at the last minute.

SERVES 4

CASSATA

Sicilian Ricotta Cake

There are two different dishes named cassata, one a cake made with ricotta and candied fruit, the other an ice-cream dessert. This cassata in its cake form is a classic Sicilian dish decorated with brightly coloured icings, marzipan and candied fruit.

400 g (14 oz) Madeira or pound cake

4 tablespoons sweet Marsala

350 g (12 oz) ricotta cheese

115 g (4 oz/½ cup) caster (superfine) sugar

½ teaspoon natural vanilla extract

150 g (5½ oz) mixed candied fruit (orange, lemon, cherries, pineapple, apricot), chopped

50 g (1¾ oz) dark chocolate, chopped

green food colouring

200 g (7 oz) marzipan

2 tablespoons apricot jam (jelly)

310 g (11 oz/2½ cups) icing (confectioners') sugar

Line a 20 cm (8 in) round cake tin with sloping sides (a moule à manqué would be perfect) with plastic wrap. Cut the cake into thin slices to line the tin, reserving enough pieces to cover the top at the end. Fit the slices of cake carefully into the tin, ensuring there are no gaps. Sprinkle the Marsala over the cake in the tin.

Beat the ricotta in a bowl until smooth. Add the caster sugar and vanilla extract and mix well. Add the candied fruit and the chocolate and mix well. Spoon into the mould, smooth the surface and cover with the remaining cake. Cover with plastic wrap and press the top down hard. Refrigerate for at least 2 hours or preferably overnight.

Unmould the cassata onto a plate. Knead enough green food colouring into the marzipan to colour it light green. Roll out the marzipan in a circle large enough to completely cover the cassata. Melt the jam in a saucepan with a tablespoon of water and brush over the cassata. Lift the marzipan over the top and trim it to fit around the edge.

Mix the icing sugar with a little hot water to make a smooth icing that will spread easily. Either pipe the icing onto the cassata in a decorative pattern, or drizzle it over the top in a crosshatch pattern.

MAKES ONE 20 CM (8 IN) CAKE

Far left: The pieces of cake need to be fitted into the mould as neatly as possible. Cut smaller pieces of cake to fill any gaps.

Left: Fill the mould with the ricotta mixture and smooth any air bubbles as you go.

Biscotti

Almond Biscuits

375 g (13 oz/3 cups) plain (all-purpose) flour
170 g (6 oz/¾ cup) caster (superfine) sugar
3 eggs

½ teaspoon baking powder
½ teaspoon natural vanilla extract
150 g (5½ oz) blanched almonds

Preheat the oven to 180°C (350°F/Gas 4) and line two baking trays with baking paper. Sift the flour into a large bowl or food processor, add the sugar, eggs, baking powder, vanilla and a pinch of salt and mix or process until you have a smooth dough. Transfer the dough to a floured surface and knead in the almonds.

Divide the dough into two pieces and roll each piece into a log about 20 cm (8 in) long. Put on the baking trays and press down gently along the top to flatten slightly. Bake for 25 minutes, or until golden. Remove the logs from the oven and leave to cool slightly while you turn the temperature down to 170°C (325°F/Gas 3).

Cut each log into 1 cm (½ in) thick diagonal slices, place on the baking tray and return to the oven for 15 minutes, or until the biscuits start to brown and are dry to the touch. Store in an airtight container.

PICTURE ON PAGE 224

MAKES 20

Amaretti

Almond Macaroons

125 g (4½ oz) blanched almonds
125 g (4½ oz) icing (confectioners') sugar
3 teaspoons plain (all-purpose) flour

2 egg whites
80 g (3 oz/⅓ cup) caster (superfine) sugar
1 teaspoon natural almond extract

Preheat the oven to 180°C (350°F/Gas 4). Put the blanched almonds, icing sugar and flour in a pestle and mortar or food processor and grind to a fine powder (be careful not to overwork the mixture or it will become oily).

Whisk the egg whites in a clean dry glass bowl until soft peaks form. Add the caster sugar a tablespoon at a time and beat continuously until you have a stiff shiny mixture. Fold in the almond mixture and the almond extract until just blended.

Spoon the mixture into a piping bag with a 1 cm (½ in) plain nozzle and pipe 3 cm (1¼ in) wide mounds, well spaced, onto a baking tray. Smooth the top of each biscuit with a damp finger and bake for 40 minutes, or until light brown. Turn off the oven, leave the door ajar and let the biscuits cool and dry out. Store in an airtight container.

PICTURE ON PAGE 224

MAKES 15

Almond Biscuits and Almond Macaroons (recipes on page 223)

Gelato al Limone

Lemon Gelato

Gelato is the Italian name for an ice cream based on an egg custard mixture, though it has now come to mean all ice creams, including sorbets. Italians are discerning about ice cream, and flavours tend to be fresh and aromatic, often based on fruit.

5 egg yolks
110 g (4 oz/½ cup) sugar
500 ml (17 fl oz/2 cups) milk

2 tablespoons grated lemon zest
3 tablespoons thick (double/heavy) cream
185 ml (6 fl oz/¾ cup) lemon juice

Whisk the egg yolks and half the sugar together until pale and creamy. Place the milk, lemon zest and remaining sugar in a saucepan and bring to the boil. Pour over the egg mixture and whisk to combine. Pour the custard back into the saucepan and cook over low heat, stirring continuously until the mixture is thick enough to coat the back of a wooden spoon – do not allow the custard to boil.

Strain the custard into a bowl. Add the cream and lemon juice and then cool over ice. Churn in an ice-cream maker following the manufacturer's instructions. Alternatively, pour the custard into a plastic freezer box, cover and freeze. Stir every 30 minutes with a whisk during freezing to break up the ice crystals and give a better texture. Keep frozen until ready to serve.

PICTURE ON OPPOSITE PAGE

SERVES 6

Gelato al Caffè

Coffee Gelato

5 egg yolks
110 g (4 oz/½ cup) sugar
500 ml (17 fl oz/2 cups) milk

125 ml (4 fl oz/½ cup) freshly made espresso
1 tablespoon Tia Maria

Whisk the egg yolks and half the sugar together until pale and creamy. Place the milk, coffee and remaining sugar in a saucepan and bring to the boil. Pour over the egg mixture and whisk to combine. Pour back into the saucepan and cook over low heat, stirring continuously until the mixture is thick enough to coat the back of a wooden spoon – do not allow the custard to boil.

Strain the custard into a bowl and cool over ice. Stir in the Tia Maria. Churn in an ice-cream maker following the manufacturer's instructions. Alternatively, pour the custard into a plastic freezer box, cover and freeze. Stir every 30 minutes with a whisk during freezing to break up the ice crystals and give a better texture. Keep frozen until ready to serve.

SERVES 6

CANNOLI

Sicilian Pastries

Ideally you should use metal cannoli tubes for this recipe. You'll find these in major department stores and speciality kitchen shops. Alternatively, you could use 2 cm (³/₄ in) wide wooden or cane doweling, cut into 12 cm (5 in) lengths.

PASTRY
155 g (5½ oz/1¼ cups) plain (all-purpose) flour
2 teaspoons cocoa powder
1 teaspoon instant coffee
1 tablespoon caster (superfine) sugar
25 g (1 oz) unsalted butter, chilled and cut
   into small cubes
3 tablespoons dry white wine
1 teaspoon dry Marsala

1 egg, beaten
oil, for deep-frying

FILLING
300 g (10½ oz) ricotta cheese
145 g (5 oz/²/₃ cup) caster (superfine) sugar
¼ teaspoon natural vanilla extract
½ teaspoon grated lemon zest
1 tablespoon candied peel, finely chopped
6 glacé cherries, chopped
15 g (½ oz) dark chocolate, grated
icing (confectioners') sugar

To make the pastry, mix the flour, cocoa powder, coffee and sugar in a bowl. Rub in the butter, then pour in the wine and Marsala and mix until the dough gathers in a loose clump. Transfer to a lightly floured surface and knead until smooth (the dough will be quite stiff). Chill in a plastic bag for 30 minutes.

Lightly dust the work surface with flour and roll the pastry out to about 32 x 24 cm (13 x 9 in). Trim the edges, then cut the pastry into twelve 8 cm (3 in) squares. Lightly oil the metal cannoli tubes. Wrap a pastry square diagonally around each tube, securing the overlapping corners with beaten egg and pressing them firmly together.

Heat the oil in a deep-fat fryer or deep frying pan to about 180°C (350°F), or until a scrap of pastry dropped into the oil becomes crisp and golden,

with a slightly blistered surface, in 15–20 seconds. If the oil starts to smoke it is too hot. Add the cannoli, a couple at a time, and deep-fry until they are golden and crisp. Remove with tongs and then drain them on paper towels. As soon as the tubes are cool enough to handle, slide them out and leave the pastries on a rack to cool.

To make the filling, mash the ricotta with a fork. Blend in the sugar and vanilla extract, then mix in the lemon zest, candied peel, glacé cherries and chocolate. Fill the pastries, either with a piping bag or a spoon. Arrange on a plate and dust with icing sugar for serving. The cannoli should be eaten soon after they are filled.

SERVES 6

COFFEE

For a country that doesn't actually produce coffee, this drink is incredibly important to Italian culture. Italians insist their coffee is prepared properly, and the rituals of making a good espresso and of café life are as important as the drink itself.

Coffee was first brought to Italy by the Arabs in the sixteenth century. By the seventeenth century, Venice had become the gateway through which the drink spread into Europe, and it was here that the beans were roasted before being dispersed throughout the Continent. As a result of the trade, coffee shops sprang up in Venice for people to enjoy this new drink and the most famous, Caffè Florian, has survived up to this day.

Caffè Florian was established in 1720 and was modelled on the coffee houses of Constantinople, which were 'schools of wisdom' for academics and literary figures. Set in a square ringed on three sides by cafés and once described by Napoleon as the Drawing Room of Europe, many of the world's most famous figures have taken coffee at Florian's while discussing art, literature and politics. Today, this historic coffee house retains its stylish elegance. Patrons can sit on the chairs stretching outside into the square, sip their cappuccinos and watch the world go by to music from the orchestra. In winter, people can choose to settle inside on one of the plush banquettes to enjoy their espressos or perhaps a grappa or Campari from the bar.

The best Italian coffee is made just from high-quality arabica beans, though some brands may be a blend of arabica and the less delicate robusta beans. For the roast, Italians tend to prefer a dark, almost burnt, roast. This gives a very concentrated flavour and aroma, and many Italians balance out the bitterness by adding sugar. Surprisingly, the darker the roast, the less caffeine, as caffeine is lost during the roasting process. Italian coffee made in bars in fact has very little caffeine, as not only does it use dark beans but also the making process is so short that the water does not come into contact with the coffee grounds for very long.

To make a coffee, the beans are freshly ground and very hot water is forced through measured amounts of this ground coffee under pressure. This produces the basic espresso – a small amount of coffee with a foamy brown crema, which can then have milk added to make a cappuccino, latte or macchiato.

In Italy, coffee is drunk in a bar (also known as a caffè bar). People visit for a cappuccino and cornetto (a croissant-shaped pastry) on their way to work, or pop in for an espresso pick-me-up in the mid-morning or afternoon, all of which are cheaper if taken standing at the bar. Ordering a caffè in Italy will always mean you get an espresso. At home, coffee is usually made in an espresso pot or moka, a double jug that boils water and forces it through the coffee grounds under pressure.

Sorbetto al Lampone

Raspberry Sorbet

Sorbets are ice creams without cream or milk. If you freeze a sorbet mixture without churning or whisking you can make a granita – the ice crystals are broken up with a fork instead for a rougher texture.

115 g (4 oz/½ cup) sugar
1 tablespoon liquid glucose or caster
  (superfine) sugar

¼ teaspoon lemon juice
200 g (7 oz) raspberries

Heat the sugar, glucose, lemon juice and 250 ml (9 fl oz/1 cup) water in a saucepan for 4 minutes, or until dissolved. Purée the raspberries in a blender or food processor or by mashing with the back of a spoon, add the syrup and process until puréed. Pass through a nylon sieve to remove the seeds.

Churn in an ice-cream maker following the manufacturer's instructions. Alternatively, pour into a plastic freezer box, cover and freeze. Stir every 30 minutes with a whisk during freezing to break up the ice crystals and give a better texture. Keep frozen until ready to serve.

PICTURE ON OPPOSITE PAGE

SERVES 4

Granita di Anguria

Watermelon Granita

450 g (1 lb) watermelon, rind and seeds removed
1 tablespoon liquid glucose or caster (superfine) sugar

½ teaspoon lemon juice

Purée the watermelon pieces in a blender or food processor, or chop it finely and push it through a metal sieve. Heat the glucose, lemon juice and 80 ml (3 fl oz/⅓ cup) water in a small saucepan for 4 minutes, or until dissolved. Add the puréed watermelon and stir well.

Pour into a plastic freezer box, cover and freeze. Stir every 30 minutes with a fork during freezing to break up the ice crystals and give a better texture. Keep frozen until ready to serve, then roughly fork to break up the ice crystals.

SERVES 4

Semifreddo al Cioccolato

Chocolate Semifreddo

500 ml (17 fl oz/2 cups) thick (double/heavy) cream
140 g (5 oz/²⁄₃ cup) caster (superfine) sugar
60 g (2¼ oz/½ cup) cocoa powder
4 eggs, separated

3 tablespoons brandy
3 tablespoons icing (confectioners') sugar
150 g (5½ oz) skinned hazelnuts, roughly chopped

Line a 1.5 litre (52 fl oz/6 cup) loaf tin with two long strips of foil. Heat 185 ml (6 fl oz/¾ cup) of the cream in a small saucepan. Combine the caster sugar, cocoa powder and egg yolks in a bowl. Pour the hot cream on top and mix well. Pour back into the saucepan and cook over low heat, stirring continuously, until the mixture is thick enough to coat the back of a wooden spoon – do not allow it to boil. Stir in the brandy and remove from the heat. Cover the surface with plastic wrap and cool for 30 minutes.

Whip the egg whites in a clean dry glass bowl until stiff peaks form. Whip the remaining cream in a large bowl until soft peaks form. Add the icing sugar and whip until stiff and glossy. Lightly fold the chocolate custard into the cream, then fold in the egg whites. Gently fold through the chopped hazelnuts. Spoon into the tin, smooth the surface and cover with foil. Freeze for at least 24 hours. Leave at room temperature for 5 minutes before serving in slices.

PICTURE ON OPPOSITE PAGE

SERVES 10

Fragole al Balsamico

Strawberries with Balsamic Vinegar

During their season, wild strawberries are abundant throughout Italy. An acidic dressing of citrus juice or red wine lifts both their flavour and aroma. In Emilia-Romagna they have been served with balsamic vinegar since Renaissance times.

500 g (1 lb 2 oz) strawberries, hulled and halved
60 ml (2 fl oz/¼ cup) good-quality balsamic vinegar
2 tablespoons caster (superfine) sugar

2 teaspoons lemon juice
3 tablespoons small mint leaves

Place the strawberries in a glass bowl. Heat the balsamic vinegar, caster sugar and lemon juice in a small saucepan, stirring until combined. Remove from the heat and leave to cool.

Pour the balsamic vinegar over the strawberries, add the mint leaves and toss together. Cover with plastic wrap and marinate in the refrigerator for at least 1 hour. Delicious served over vanilla ice cream.

SERVES 6

Panforte

Siena Cake

Panforte means 'strong bread', an apt description for this dense, fruity loaf that still retains its medieval flavour. Panforte is also known as Siena cake – Siena possibly being the first Italian city to use sugar and spices such as white pepper.

105 g (3½ oz/¾ cup) hazelnuts
115 g (4 oz/¾ cup) almonds
125 g (4½ oz) candied mixed peel, chopped
100 g (3½ oz) candied pineapple, chopped
grated zest of 1 lemon
80 g (3 oz/⅔ cup) plain (all-purpose) flour
1 teaspoon ground cinnamon
¼ teaspoon ground coriander
¼ teaspoon ground cloves
¼ teaspoon grated nutmeg
pinch of white pepper
140 g (5 oz/⅔ cup) sugar
4 tablespoons honey
50 g (1¾ oz) unsalted butter
icing (confectioners') sugar

Line a 23 cm (9 in) springform tin with rice paper or baking paper and grease well with butter. Toast the nuts under a hot grill (broiler), turning them so they brown on all sides, then leave to cool. Put the nuts in a bowl with the mixed peel, pineapple, lemon zest, flour and spices and toss together. Preheat the oven to 150°C (300°F/Gas 2).

Put the sugar, honey and butter in a saucepan and stir until melted. Cook the syrup until it reaches 120°C (250°F) on a sugar thermometer, or a little of it dropped into cold water forms a soft ball when moulded between your finger and thumb.

Pour the hot syrup into the nut mixture and mix well, working fast before it stiffens too much. Pour straight into the tin, smooth the surface and bake for 35 minutes. (Unlike other cakes, this one will neither firm up as it cooks or colour at all so you need to time it carefully.)

Cool in the tin until the cake firms up enough to remove the side of the tin. Peel off the paper and leave to cool completely. Dust the top heavily with icing sugar.

MAKES ONE 23 CM (9 IN) CAKE

BASICS

An important step in mastering any cuisine is learning the basic recipes and techniques. Straight from the recipe journal, here are the ones no Italian cook would be without.

Pasta

500 g (1 lb 2 oz) 00 (doppio zero) or plain
  (all-purpose) flour

4 eggs
chilled water

Mound the flour on a work surface or in a large bowl. Make a well in the centre. Break the eggs into the well and whisk with a fork, incorporating the flour as you whisk. You may need to add a little chilled water (1/4 teaspoon at a time) to make a loosely massed dough. Turn the dough onto a lightly floured surface – it should be soft, pliable and dry to the touch. Knead for 6–8 minutes, or until smooth and elastic with a slightly glossy appearance. Cover with a tea towel and leave for 30 minutes. The dough is then ready to roll out.

To make the dough in a processor, mix the flour for 2–3 seconds, then add the eggs with the motor running. Mix again for 5 seconds, or until the mixture looks like coarse meal. Mix until a loose ball forms, then continue for 4–5 seconds until the machine slows and stops. If the dough seems too sticky to form a smooth ball, add 2 teaspoons flour, mix briefly and continue adding small amounts of flour until the ball forms. If the mixture is too dry, add chilled water, a teaspoon at a time. Transfer to a lightly floured surface and knead for 2–3 minutes until smooth and elastic. Cover with a tea towel and leave for 30 minutes.

To roll out the dough, divide into two or three manageable portions. Work with one portion at a time, keeping the rest covered. Flatten the dough onto a lightly floured surface and roll out from the centre to the outer edge, rotating the dough often. When you have a 5 mm (1/4 in) thick circle, fold the dough in half and roll it out again. Do this eight times to give a smooth circle of pasta, then roll to a thickness of 2.5 mm (1/8 in). (Mend any tears with a little pasta from the outside of the circle and a little water.) Transfer to a lightly floured tea towel. If the pasta is to be filled, keep it covered and don't allow it to dry out. If the sheets are to be cut into lengths or shapes, leave them uncovered while you roll out the other portions, so the surface moisture will dry slightly before cutting.

If you have a pasta machine, work the dough through the rollers, making the setting smaller each time until the dough is the correct thickness.

MAKES 700 G (1 LB 9 OZ)

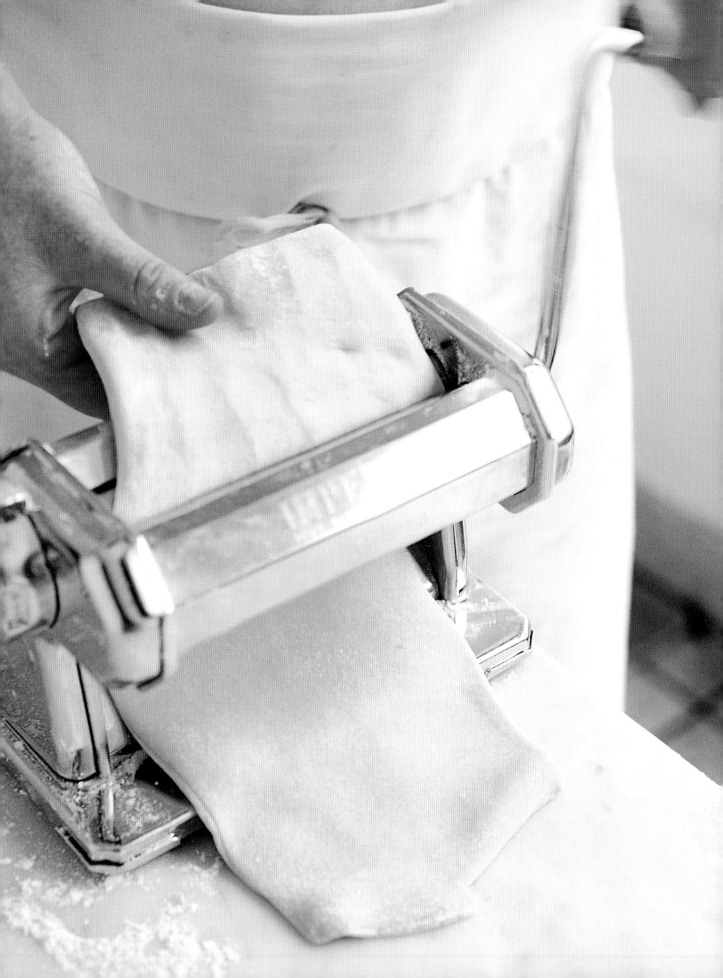

Sugo di Pomodoro
Tomato Sauce

120 g (4 oz) Roma (plum) tomatoes
3 basil leaves
2 garlic cloves, crushed

1 tablespoon tomato passata
2 teaspoons extra virgin olive oil

Core the tomatoes and purée in a food processor with the basil leaves (or chop the tomatoes and basil very finely and stir together). Stir in the garlic, passata and olive oil and season well.

Leave for at least 30 minutes before serving to allow the flavours to blend. Use on pizzas, toss through pasta or serve with arancini or supplì.

MAKES 185 ML (6 FL OZ/³⁄4 CUP)

Besciamella
Béchamel Sauce

65 g (2 oz) butter
40 g (1½ oz/⅓ cup) plain (all-purpose) flour
pinch of grated nutmeg

610 ml (20 fl oz/2¼ cups) milk
1 bay leaf

Heat the butter in a saucepan over low heat. Add the flour and grated nutmeg and cook, stirring, for 1 minute. Remove from the heat and gradually stir in the milk. Add the bay leaf, return the pan to the heat and simmer, stirring often, until the sauce thickens. Season, then cover with plastic wrap to prevent a skin forming, and cool. Discard the bay leaf before using.

MAKES 810 ML (29 FL OZ/3¼ CUPS)

PASTA PER PIZZA
Pizza Dough

1 tablespoon caster (superfine) sugar
2 teaspoons dried yeast or 15 g (1/2 oz) fresh yeast
215 ml (7 fl oz) lukewarm water
450 g (1 lb/3²/₃ cups) plain (all-purpose) flour

1/2 teaspoon salt
3 tablespoons olive oil
cornmeal

Put the sugar and yeast in a small bowl and stir in 90 ml (3 fl oz) of the water. Leave in a draught-free spot to activate. If the yeast does not bubble and foam in 5 minutes, discard it and start again.

Mix the flour and salt in a bowl or a food processor fitted with a plastic blade. Add the oil, remaining water and the yeast mixture. Mix until the dough loosely clumps together. Transfer it to a lightly floured surface and knead for 8 minutes, adding a little flour or warm water if necessary, until you have a soft dough that is not sticky but is dry to the touch.

Rub the inside of a large bowl with oil. Roll the ball of dough around in the bowl to coat it with oil, then cut a shallow cross on the top of the ball with a sharp knife. Leave the dough in the bowl, cover with a tea towel or put in a plastic bag and leave in a draught-free spot for 1–1½ hours until doubled in size (or leave in the refrigerator for 8 hours to rise slowly).

Punch down the dough to its original size, then divide into two portions. (At this stage the dough can be stored in the refrigerator for up to 4 hours, or frozen. Bring back to room temperature before continuing.)

Working with one portion at a time, push the dough out to make a thick circle. Using the heels of your hands and working from the centre of the circle outwards, flatten the dough into a 30 cm (12 in) circle with a slightly raised rim. (If you find it difficult to push the dough out by hand you can use a rolling pin.) The dough is now ready to use, as instructed in the recipe. Cook on a lightly oiled tray, dusted with cornmeal, and get it into the oven as quickly as possible.

MAKES TWO 30 CM (12 IN) PIZZA BASES

Pasta per Focaccia
Focaccia Dough

½ teaspoon caster (superfine) sugar
2 teaspoons dried yeast or 15 g (½ oz) fresh yeast
810 ml (29 fl oz/3¼ cups) lukewarm water
1 kg (2 lb 4 oz) plain (all-purpose) flour

2 teaspoons salt
2 tablespoons olive oil
cornmeal

Put the caster sugar and yeast in a small bowl and stir in 60 ml (2 fl oz/¼ cup) of the water. Leave in a draught-free spot to activate. If the yeast does not bubble and foam in 5 minutes, discard it and start again.

Mix the flour and salt in a bowl or a food processor fitted with a plastic blade. Add the olive oil, the yeast mixture and three-quarters of the remaining water. Mix, then add the rest of the water, a little at a time, until the dough loosely clumps together. Transfer to a lightly floured surface and knead for 8 minutes until smooth, or until the impression made by a finger springs back immediately.

Rub the inside of a large bowl with oil. Roll the ball of dough around in the bowl to coat it with oil, then cut a shallow cross on the top of the ball with a sharp knife. Leave the dough in the bowl, cover with a tea towel or put in a plastic bag and leave in a draught-free spot for 1–1½ hours until doubled in size (or leave in the refrigerator for 8 hours to rise slowly).

Punch down the dough to its original size, then divide it into two portions. (At this stage the dough can be refrigerated for 4 hours, or frozen. Bring it back to room temperature before continuing.) Roll each portion of dough out to a 28 x 20 cm (11 x 8 in) rectangle, then use the heels of your hands, working from the centre of the dough outwards, to make a 38 x 28 cm (15 x 11 in) rectangle.

Lightly oil 2 baking trays and dust with cornmeal. Put a portion of dough in the centre of each tray and press out to fill the tray. Slide the trays inside a plastic bag. Seal and leave in a draught-free spot for 2 hours to rise again. The focaccia dough is now ready to use, as instructed in the recipe.

MAKES 2 FOCACCIA

Pesto

Pesto Sauce

2 garlic cloves
50 g (2 oz/⅓ cup) pine nuts
80 g (3 oz/1⅔ cups) basil leaves

4 tablespoons grated Parmesan
150 ml (5 fl oz) extra virgin olive oil

Put the garlic, pine nuts, basil and Parmesan in a mortar and pestle or a food processor and pound or mix to a paste. Add the oil in a steady stream, mixing continuously. Season with salt if necessary. Refrigerate in a sterilized jar, covered with a layer of olive oil, for up to 3 weeks.

MAKES 185 ML (6 FL OZ/¾ CUP)

Salsa Verde

Green Sauce

1½ tablespoons fresh white breadcrumbs
1 tablespoon milk
1 hard-boiled egg yolk
2 anchovy fillets
1 tablespoon capers

5 tablespoons finely chopped flat-leaf (Italian) parsley, mint and basil
1 garlic clove, crushed
80 ml (3 fl oz/⅓ cup) extra virgin olive oil

Soak the breadcrumbs in the milk for 10 minutes. Finely chop together the egg yolk, anchovy and capers. Add the herbs, garlic and breadcrumb mixture and mix with a fork. Slowly blend in the oil until smooth and thick. Season with pepper, then set aside for at least 1 hour before using.

MAKES 185 ML (6 FL OZ/¾ CUP)

Vinaigrette al Limone

Vinaigrette

2 tablespoons lemon juice
4 tablespoons olive oil
1 tablespoon chopped parsley

2 teaspoons finely chopped onion or 1 finely chopped
    French shallot

Make the dressing by combining all the
ingredients. Season with salt and pepper.

MAKES 180 ML (6 FL OZ)

Pomodori al Forno

Oven-dried Tomatoes

24 Roma (plum) tomatoes
sea salt
4 garlic cloves, crushed
1/2 tablespoon extra virgin olive oil

24 basil leaves
1 mild red chilli, cut into 24 small pieces
1/2 tablespoon dried oregano
750 ml (27 fl oz/3 cups) olive oil

Preheat the oven to 75°C (150°F/Gas 1/4). Core
each Roma tomato and slice almost in half along
its length, with just the skin keeping it together.
Open out butterfly-fashion and space out, cut-side
up, on wire racks. Sprinkle with sea salt and bake
for about 8 hours, until dark and almost leathery,
but not crisp. Cool and store in sterilized jars for
up to six months, or preserve as below.

Mix the crushed garlic with the extra virgin olive
oil. Brush one half of each tomato, then place a
basil leaf, piece of chilli and sprinkling of oregano
on top. Fold the other half over to enclose and
place in a sterilized jar. Pour in the olive oil to
cover the tomatoes and push down firmly to expel
any air. Seal and refrigerate for up to two months.

FILLS A 2 LITRE (70 FL OZ/8 CUP) JAR

GLOSSARY

AL DENTE
Meaning 'to the tooth'. Pasta and risotto rice are cooked until al dente – the outside is tender but the centre still has a little resistance or 'bite'.

AMARETTI
Small biscuits like macaroons, made from sweet and bitter almonds.

ARTICHOKE (carciofo)
The edible flower of a member of the thistle family. Some have thorns and the types vary in size. The largest are usually boiled, but the smallest and most tender can be eaten raw.

BOCCONCINI
Means literally 'small mouthful' and generally refers to small balls of mozzarella cheese.

BOUQUET GARNI
A bundle of herbs used to flavour dishes. Made by tying sprigs of parsley, thyme, celery leaves and a bay leaf in muslin or a portion of leek.

BRESAOLA
Lean beef that has been cured and air-dried for 2–3 months – a speciality of the Valtellina Valley in Lombardia. Serve thinly sliced.

CANTUCCI
Tuscan almond biscuits, also known as biscotti di Prato. They are usually eaten dipped into a dessert wine such as vin santo.

CAPERBERRIES
The fruit of the caper bush. They are usually served as an accompaniment, like olives.

CAPERS
The pickled flowers of the caper bush. These are available preserved in brine, vinegar or salt. Rinse well and squeeze dry before use.

CARDOONS
Similar to the artichoke plant, cardoons have large leaves and long stems, and it is the stems that are eaten.

CASALINGA
Means 'home-made' or 'homely'. When attributed to sausages or salami, it generally means having a coarse texture and earthy flavour.

CAVOLO NERO
Cabbage with long leaves that are so dark green they appear to be almost black. If unavailable, Savoy cabbage can be used.

CETRIOLINI
Small gherkins. If unavailable, use cornichons or small cocktail gherkins.

CIABATTA
Slipper-shaped Italian bread with a rough, open texture. Ciabatta quickly goes stale and is best eaten on the day it is bought or made.

CIPOLLINE
Small white onions, usually flattened in appearance rather than round.

COPPA
A type of cured pork made from half pork fat and half pig's neck and shoulder. It is rolled and cured in a casing and resembles a fatty sausage.

COTECHINO

A sausage made from pork and pork rind, giving it a gelatinous texture. It is flavoured with cloves and cinnamon. It must be cooked before eating.

COUNTRY-STYLE BREAD

Any bread that is bought as a whole loaf and has a rough texture, such as pugliese, ciabatta and pane Toscano. Other white bread is not a suitable substitute.

CROCCANTE

Caramelized nuts, usually almonds but sometimes hazelnuts (also known as pralines).

DOPPIO ZERO (00) FLOUR

The finest grade of flour, made from soft wheat (grano tenero) and mainly used for making cakes and fresh egg pasta.

FARRO

A type of spelt grain, used in soups and stews. If unavailable, spelt or barley can be used.

FINOCCHIONA

A type of salami from Tuscany, flavoured with wild fennel seeds.

FLAT-LEAF PARSLEY

Also known as Italian or continental parsley. Used as an ingredient rather than a garnish.

FONTINA

A traditional mountain cheese. Full-fat and semi-soft with a sweetish flavour, fontina melts well and so is particularly good for cooking.

GORGONZOLA

A blue cheese, originally made in Gorgonzola in Lombardia. It melts well and is used in sauces. If not available, use another full-fat blue cheese.

JUNIPER BERRIES

Blackish-purple berries with a resin flavour. Used in stews and game dishes. Crush the berries slightly to release their flavour.

MARSALA

A fortified wine from Marsala in Sicily. It comes in varying degrees of dryness and sweetness. Dry Marsalas are used in savoury dishes, and sweet ones in desserts.

MASCARPONE

A cream cheese originally from Lombardia. Made with cream, it is very high in fat and is generally used in desserts such as tiramisù or instead of cream in sauces.

MISTICANZA

A Roman salad that was once made of wild greens. Today it is a mixture of rocket (arugula), purslane, sorrel, mint, dandelion, wild fennel and endive with some lettuce. In Umbria it also refers to a mixture of dried beans used for soups.

MORTADELLA

A large, finely textured pork sausage, with lengths of lard running through it. Some versions contain pistachio nuts. Traditionally made in Bologna, the sausage is also known as bologna or boloney in the USA.

OLIVE

Olives can be named after where they come from, such as Ligurian; their curing style, such as Sicilian; or their variety, such as Cerignola. Though green and black olives have a different flavour, they can be used interchangeably in recipes unless the final colour is a factor.

OLIVE OIL

Extra virgin and virgin olive oils are pressed without any heat or chemicals and are best used in simple uncooked dishes and for salads. Pure olive oil can be used for cooking or deep-frying.

PANCETTA

Cured belly of pork, somewhat like streaky bacon. Available in flat pieces or rolled up (arrotolata), and both smoked and unsmoked. Generally used, either sliced or cut into cubes, as an ingredient in dishes like spaghetti carbonara.

PARMA HAM

This prosciutto has a sweet taste and is flavoured only with salt. Parma hams can be identified by the stamp on the skin showing the five-pointed star of the Dukes of Parma. Other prosciutto can be used if Parma ham is unavailable.

PASSATA

Meaning 'puréed', this most commonly refers to a smooth uncooked tomato pulp bought in tins or jars.

PECORINO

One of Italy's most popular cheeses, virtually every region produces a version. Made from sheep's milk and always by the same method, although the result varies according to the milk and ageing process used.

PEPERONCINI

The Italian name for chillies, these are popular in the cooking of the South, and are also served there as a condiment.

POLENTA

The name of the dish and the ingredient itself, which is ground corn. The cornmeal comes in different grades of coarseness. Finer varieties are used in cakes and coarse ones accompany stews.

PORCINI

The Italian name for a cep or boletus mushroom. Usually bought dried and reconstituted in boiling water, but available fresh in the spring and autumn.

PROSCIUTTO

Italian name for ham. Prosciutto crudo is cured ham and includes Parma ham and San Daniele. Prosciutto cotto is cooked ham.

PROVOLONE

Curd cheese made from cows' milk. The curds are spun and worked into large pear- or tube-shaped cheeses, then immersed in brine and bound with string. Available fresh or matured and eaten as a table cheese or used in cooking.

RADICCHIO

A salad leaf of the chicory family with slightly bitter red leaves. There are several varieties.

RISOTTO RICE

Round-grained, very absorbent rice, cultivated in northern Italy. Risotto rice comes in four categories, classified by the size of each grain.

SOFFRITTO

A flavour base for soups, stews and risottos. Soffritto is a mixture of fried ingredients like onion, celery, carrot, garlic, pancetta and herbs. It means literally to 'under-fry' and the mixture should be sweated rather than coloured.

SQUID/CUTTLEFISH INK

Used to colour and flavour pasta and risotto. The ink is stored in a sac that can be removed from whole squid and cuttlefish or bought in sachets from fishmongers or delicatessens.

TALEGGIO

A mountain cheese originally from the Italian Alps near Bergamo, but now also made in other regions. Taleggio is a very good table and cooking cheese and should be eaten young as its flavour becomes more acidic with age. It is made in squares and has a pink-yellow crust and a creamy centre.

TRUFFLES

Black truffles and white truffles can be found in Italy. The black ones come from Umbria, Piemonte and Emilia-Romagna. The white ones come from Alba, Emilia-Romagna, Le Marche, Tuscany and Umbria. Truffles are very expensive but only a tiny amount is needed. Preserved truffles and truffle oil are also available.

VIN SANTO

A golden dessert wine eaten with cantucci biscuits. Now made all over Italy, but the best known is made in Tuscany.

ZUCCHINI

The Italian name for courgettes.

INDEX

Published in 2010 by Murdoch Books Pty Limited

Murdoch Books Australia
Pier 8/9, 23 Hickson Road
Millers Point NSW 2000
Phone: +61 (0)2 8220 2000
Fax: +61 (0)2 8220 2558
www.murdochbooks.com.au

Murdoch Books UK Limited
Erico House, 6th Floor
93–99 Upper Richmond Road
Putney, London SW15 2TG
Phone: +44 (0)20 8785 5995
Fax: +44 (0)20 8785 5985
www.murdochbooks.co.uk

Chief Executive: Juliet Rogers
Publishing Director: Kay Scarlett

Publisher: Lynn Lewis
Senior Designer: Heather Menzies
Series Design Concept: Sarah Odgers
Photographer: Alan Benson, Natasha Milne, Ashley Mackevicus,
Prue Roscoe, Ian Hofsetter and Martin Brigdale
Project Editor: Justine Harding
Designer: Susanne Geppert
Index: Jo Rudd

ISBN: 978-1-74266-104-9

PRINTED IN CHINA.

IMPORTANT: Those who might be at risk from the effects of salmonella poisoning (the elderly, pregnant women, young children
and those suffering from immune deficiency diseases) should consult their doctor with any concerns about eating raw eggs.

OVEN GUIDE: You may find cooking times vary depending on the oven you are using. For fan-forced ovens, as a general rule,
set the oven temperature to 20°C (35°F) lower than indicated in the recipe.